The Parallel Universe of English

佐藤良明/柴田元幸——[編]

東京大学出版会

The Parallel Universe of English
Yoshiaki SATO and Motoyuki SHIBATA, Editors
University of Tokyo Press, 1996
ISBN 4–13–082102–4

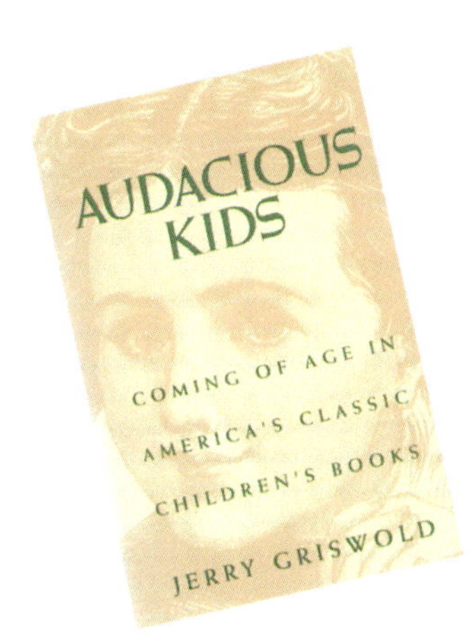

the coast of
chicago

STUART DYBEK

David Blair, from *Lost Tribes*
CG by Florence Ormezzano

Norman Conquest
(Derek Pell),
"Weird Romance"

old
ways
to
fold New Paper

poems by Leza Lowitz

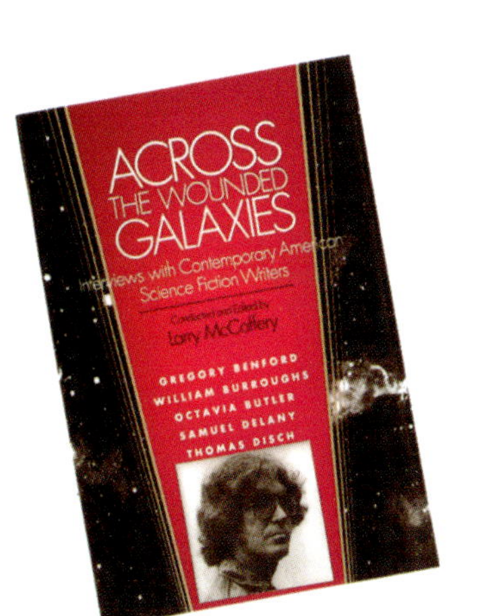

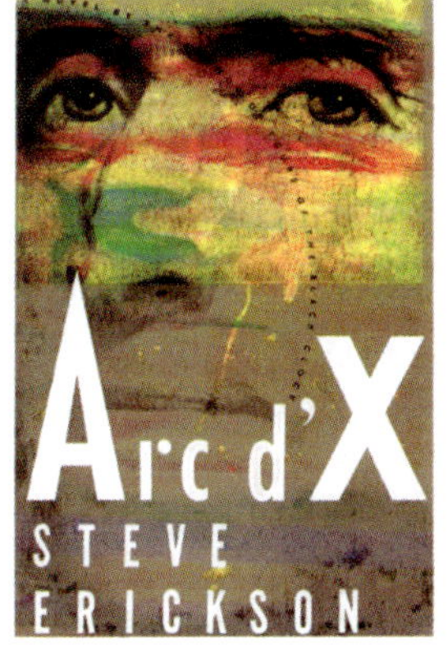

Paul Alkebulan with Yoshiaki Sato (1981)

Steve Erickson with Motoyuki Shibata (1993)
Photo by Yasuhide Kuge

The Parallel Universe of English

まえがき(の・ようなもの)

現代日本の演劇を論じた内野儀(ただし)の快著『メロドラマの逆襲』(勁草書房)に，英語教育について触れた一節がある．まず内野儀は，近年の大学英語教育でよく言われる2つの議論を要約してみせる．ひとつは，「現状批判型」．最近の学生は知的関心をもたず，せっかく教師が熱心にはたらきかけてもそれを受け入れる素養がない，ああ，嘆かわしい....もうひとつは「現状肯定型」．ほとんどの学生が企業に就職するのだから，大学でも「役に立つ」英語を教えるのは当然である....「そしてぼくは，そのどちらにも違和感を覚える」と記した上で，内野儀はこう書く．

> ことは至極単純なことで，たとえば，学生たちの顔を授業中に凝視するだけで事足りる．そのときぼくたち英語教師は，何を教えてよいのかわからないという事実を前にして，そしてまた，教育などというものをはなから信じていない学生たちを前にして，まずはおびえ，たじろぐはずなのだ．教育を信じることを強要することなどできはしない．どうすれば教育が成立するのか，問題はそれしかない．ただしそれは，理念の問題ではなく実践の問題である．あらたな教育の理念ではなく，きわめて現場的な戦略と方法がまずは考えられねばならない．そしてそれは，これまでの英語教育をめぐるあらゆる理念はもはや失効しているという認識から生み出されなければならない．何を教えるのかは，そのあとに問われてくる問題である．

教育をめぐる，これ以上正しい議論を僕は知らない．

教えるということを少しでも真面目に考える教師なら，みんなかならず「内なる内野儀」を抱えているはずである．自分は何の権利をもって，この教材をこの人たちに「教えて」いるのか．いかなる理由で，春の日の気持ちのいい午後に，何十人もの人々を薄暗い建物のなかに監禁していることを自分は正当化できるのか．

教養を強要することはできないし，共用することもできない．にもかかわらず，教養学部なんていう名前のところで，「何を教えてよいのかわか」っているような顔してふるまうのは，けっこう疲れる．

本書 *The Parallel Universe of English* は，そういう「疲れ」をこの場に限り免除してもらって作ったアンソロジーである．授業で共用することを意図せず，誰にも強要しないことを前提にしているぶん，ほんの少し気が楽である．僕はこの本で何を「教える」こともめざしていない．ここに収めたのは，僕と佐藤さんの友人たちが書き下ろしてくれたものを中心とする，楽しかったり刺激的だったり笑わせられたりジンときたりする(要するに，何らかの意味で読んで損はないように思える)文章だが，ここで僕はその内容の素晴らしさをことさらに宣伝したり，外国語を読むことの知的楽しさを謳いあげたりすることは控えたいと思う．代わりに，内田百閒の童話集『王様の背中』の「序」から引用して終わりたい．「この本のお話には，教訓はなんにも含まれて居りませんから，皆さんは安心して読んで下さい」．🅛

そんなことないよ，ここにだってずいぶん教訓はある，とつむじ曲がりの佐藤君が口を挟む．——人生は愉快な方がいい．考えは自由な方がいい．感性は細やかな方がいいし，感覚がぶっとんでいるのは，それはそれでまた愉しい．本も映画もいいものはいいし，いい友達はもっといい．．．．

試験も成績も単位も改革も運営も視察も理念も弁明も何もない，現実をすり抜けたところに夢見た「パラレルな宇宙」が，東大出版会の後藤健介さんをはじめとする方々のセンスによって，こういう形で実現した．15人の私的な声が，ちょっとした物語とともに，ときどき奇妙にハモりながら，英語でそこにただよっているという，ただそれだけのアンソロジーだから，どこでも面白そうなところから入っていってくだされればと思う．パラパラ読みたい人にも，レルレル(?)と文字を追っていきたい人にもいいように，なにかと「註」をつけたけれど，今読み返すと僕らはただ右のページで，お囃しを入れていただけじゃないかという気がしないでもない．🅢

Contents

Rust Never Sleeps

The Times They Are A-Changing?

Human Touch, Post-Human Caress

Rust Never Sleeps

SESSION 1

Confessions of a Radio Junkie

■

Joseph Hoffmann

I ADMIT IT, I'M a radio junkie. I've been addicted to radio ever since I was a kid. When I was about eight or nine years old, I — like most of the other boys I knew then — used to hide a small transistor radio under my pillow at night, so that I could listen to sports broadcasts after I was supposed to be asleep. I [5] would listen to baseball games in the summer, and basketball games in the winter. Many times, I would wake up in the morning to find the radio still on and the batteries dead. Or, worse yet, to find the radio on the floor at the side of the bed, broken into pieces. I went through lots of batteries, and lots of radios. [10]

When I grew up and graduated from college, I was lucky enough to find a job as a radio announcer. I learned a lot about the radio business during the three years that I was a part of it.

I worked for both small-town and large-city radio stations. In small towns, I learned, radio is more than just entertainment; it is [15] a vital part of the community. In fact, in many American small towns, radio is the major — and perhaps the only — source of local news and information.

A small-town radio station is a source of local pride, and everyone who works there is a local celebrity. I didn't realize this until [20] the time I was stuck "on the air" during a flood. I was working at a station that was situated on a hill at the bend of a river. That

法学専攻のジョゼフ・ホフマン教授(インディアナ大)は元ラジオのディスクジョッキー．フルブライト交換教授として東京大学で教えたこともある．今回書いてもらったのは，DJ 時代の体験を綴った軽快な文章．まさに気持ちのいいラジオ番組のノリである．Ⓛ

Confessions of a Radio Junkie: Confessions of . . . といえば，古典的なところではトマス・ド・クィンシーの *Confessions of an English Opium Eater* (『阿片常用者の告白』1822) が思い浮かぶ．Junkie といえばふつうは麻薬常用者のことで，「麻薬文学」の帝王ウィリアム・バロウズの最初の小説 (1953) のタイトルでもあるが，そういえばその副題も *Confessions of an Unredeemed Drug Addict* (救いなきドラッグ中毒者の告白) だった．ホフマン教授のラジオ好きには，こうした危ない世界に近いものがあるというわけ．

[10] went through: go through は「～を使い果たす」. *John goes through a lot of beer while watching baseball on TV.*
[16] vital: extremely important; very necessary
[20] a local celebrity: 地元の名士
[21] was stuck "on the air": 「オンエア」の状態に閉じこめられてしまった
[22] bend: 曲がり目

spring, the river flooded, and the station was soon cut off from the
rest of the town. I was stranded at the station for almost twenty-
four hours, until my relief announcer could be brought in by rowboat. While I was stuck "on the air," I kept myself awake and alert
by describing how the rising flood waters were gradually ap- [5]
proaching the station's front door. I really didn't think anyone
was paying any attention to me, especially because the flood was
causing trouble for everyone in town.

After my substitute finally arrived, the first thing I did was
head for the nearest grocery store to buy some food. When I [10]
reached the checkout line, a group of excited people gathered
around me. "Weren't you worried?" "How did you manage it?"
"We're all so relieved that you're OK!" I didn't know any of them,
but they all seemed to know me. My description of the rising
flood waters had apparently turned into a real-life drama for [15]
many radio listeners in town. The experience taught me about the
power of the medium — from that day on, I was always con-
scious of the fact that radio connects powerfully with people, and
of the responsibility that this placed upon me as a radio announcer. [20]

Radio, whether in a small town or a large city, connects with
people in ways that television does not. Radio is a near-constant
presence, almost like a best friend, to many people. It provides a
kind of "soundtrack" for people's daily lives. Unlike television,
which tends to take people away from other activities, radio — at [25]
least most of time — operates in the background. People can con-
tinue to work, play, and converse with others while they are listening to the radio.

In some ways, small-town stations and stations in larger cities
are quite different. For example, in small towns, everyone listens [30]
to the local station, no matter what. So small-town programming
tends to follow a "shotgun" strategy — each hour of the day, a
different kind of programming will be offered. One hour, a small-
town station might play country-and-western music; the next
hour, religious music; and the next hour, maybe rock-and-roll [35]

[2] was stranded: 取り残された

[3] rowboat: boatは日本語のかなり大きな「船」も指すので，いわゆる「ボート」の意味であることをはっきりさせる場合にはこう言う.

[4] alert: 気の張った状態.

[9] substitute: 3行目の relief announcer のこと.

[10] head for: ～へ向かう

[11] checkout line: レジの列

[17] the medium: (ラジオという)メディア. 日本語ではもっぱら複数形で「メディア」というが，単数は medium.

[27] converse: to talk

[32] a "shotgun" strategy: 以下を読めばわかるように，この shotgun は「散弾銃」のイメージ. 関係ないが，女性が妊娠してやむをえずする結婚を shotgun marriage という(女の子の父親が男にショットガンをつきつけているイメージ). もっと関係ないが，女の子が「じゃーまーいいか」と妥協的態度で決める結婚を Jamaica marriage という(嘘).

music. The idea is to offer lots of different kinds of programming to suit everyone's different tastes.

In larger markets, however, a "shotgun" strategy is suicidal. This is because radio, unlike television, is a "tune-out" rather than a "tune-in" medium. With television, people will look in the [5] TV guide to find a particular program they want to watch at a particular time. And they will turn to whatever channel is offering that particular program. With radio, people do just the opposite — they tend to leave their radio tuned to a particular station until they hear something they DON'T want to listen to, and then [10] they switch to a different station. In larger markets, therefore, where people have a choice of many different local radio stations, a station that follows a "shotgun" strategy winds up with no listeners at all — by the end of each day, everyone will have "tuned out" to some other station that offers a more consistent dose of [15] their favorite kind of programming. That's why stations in larger cities tend to look for special programming "niches," that aren't being served consistently by any other station.

Another difference between small-town and large-city stations is that, in small towns, news and sports reporters can afford to be [20] nice to the people they report about. Small-town news reporters, for example, can get away with reporting mostly "good news." And sportscasters in small towns can root for the home teams; it's okay — actually, it's practically required — to be a local "booster." After all, everybody else in the town is also cheering [25] for the home team (usually, the local high school). You've got to try to be objective, but you certainly don't want to be too critical. In big cities, on the other hand, the trend is to be an "investigative reporter." Like Woodward and Bernstein, everybody wants to break a big scandal, or at least a negative story. "What was the [30] REAL reason for the mayor missing that meeting last night?" "Why didn't the basketball coach call a timeout before that last shot?" News and sports reporters for large-city stations have to be rough and tough — they can't be too friendly with the subjects of their reports. [35]

[3] suicidal: 自殺行為の

[4] "tune-out" . . . "tune-in": ここで分からなくても以下を読めばわかる. まずは read on.

[7] particular: 「特別の」と覚えている人が多いが, ここの場合のように「特定の」の意になることの方がずっと多い(次, 次々行の particular も同様).

[13] winds up with no listeners at all: 結局1人も聴取者がいなくなってしまう

[15] a more consistent dose: 直訳すれば「もっと一貫した(薬の)投与」. ジャンキーのメタファーがまたちょっと顔を出す.

[17] "niche(s)": これはエコロジー(生態学)のメタファー.「ニッチ」あるいは「生態的地位」, つまり種それぞれの生育場所・地位.

[22] can get away with . . . : 「〜しても許される」. *How can he be so rude to his boss and get away with it?*

[23] root for . . . : 〜を応援する

[24] practically: 事実上

[25] "booster": 後援者, 熱狂的支持者

[27] don't want to . . . : 〜するのはまずい

[28] "investigative reporter": 犯罪・汚職などに関して独自の調査による報道を行なう記者.

[29] Woodward and Bernstein: "investigative reporting" のもっとも有名な例といえるウォーターゲート事件報道で名を上げた,『ワシントン・ポスト』の記者.

For me, one of the strangest things about working in radio was the fact that radio was, at the same time, both an impersonal and an intensely personal medium. For a radio announcer, radio can be very impersonal. The communication that occurs on the radio, after all, is almost entirely one-way; and the announcer is usually [5] alone in the radio station, surrounded only by machines. But radio is also intensely personal, because that is how radio listeners tend to experience it. Even though you know it isn't so, as a radio listener, it's easy to believe that the announcer is talking directly to you, on a one-to-one basis. That's why almost all radio an- [10] nouncers, sooner or later, encounter "groupies" — listeners (usually of the opposite sex) who develop a fixation on them, and try to become a part of their personal lives. It's sad, but it's also understandable.

Today, unfortunately, the "personal" side of radio seems to be [15] disappearing. Many radio stations, to cut costs, are switching to automation. The programming is done by computer — all the announcer has to do is pre-record the song intros, public service announcements, and even time checks. The order of the songs is determined by the computer, rather than by a human disk jockey [20] who is striving to "blend" consecutive songs into a tapestry of compatible sounds and moods. The computer has no musical taste — and it also never makes mistakes. Every segue is the same; each song overlaps the one before and after it by the same period of five seconds. [25]

As a former radio announcer, and a lifelong radio junkie, I bemoan the shift from human disk jockeys to computer automation. The computer can't connect with me in the way that a good DJ can. That's why, when I'm listening to the radio, I am often pleased to hear a particularly "rough" segue, or maybe even a [30] few seconds of "dead air" between songs. It tells me that I'm listening to a station operated by a real human being, and not by a computer.

[12] develop a fixation on them : アナウンサーに(なかば病的に)夢中になる

[18] public service announcements : 来月よりバスが増便になります，工事のため一部地域でガスが止まります，といった公的な「お知らせ」.

[21] consecutive songs : 続いてかかる曲. *That song stayed No. 1 in six consecutive weeks.*

a tapestry of compatible sounds and moods : 無理なく溶けあった音とムードのつづれ織り

[23] segue : [ségwei] 元々は音楽用語で，断絶なく次の楽章に移れという指示.

[26] bemoan : 悲しむ，嘆く

SESSION 2

Love Child

■

Shyana Quasha

MY NAME IS Shyana. It may not seem like such an odd name, but to an elementary school child surrounded by biblically named Marys, Josephs, and a fair assortment of Peters and Pauls, it was definitely a cross to bear. Teachers would go out of their way to mispronounce it, to which I would parrot my [5] mother's words: "it's phonetic!" Later, I entered a Montessori school where my name seemed conservative on a roll sheet that included Rainbow Johnson, Wind Turnbull, and my good friend "O."

We were the children of rebellious people, people who chose [10] their children's names as a response to the ancestral names they themselves were saddled with. My name had its own story, but I'll come back to that later.

As a child born in San Francisco's Summer of Love, there were certain things expected. I did indeed wear tie-dyed, macraméd, [15] crocheted and, above all, hand-made clothing. On one notable occasion, my parents and me graced the pages of the local paper decked out in matching fringed suede coats. The first store-bought pair of shoes that I remember choosing by myself were a pair of white vinyl go-go boots. Scraps of velour and silver lamé [20] from my mother's designs filled the quilt on my crib, and later accented the Mother/Daughter ensembles we wore. True, the

シャイアナ・クアシャは，大学講師になったSteveと結婚として今岐阜に住んでいる．仕事はフォトグラフィック・アーティスト．1967年の花のサンフランシスコ，というのはぼくのポップ心のふるさとなわけで，そのときその地で生まれたシャイアナは，もうそれだけであまりに眩しいのに，ジャニス当人のナマの「サマータイム」を子守歌に聞いていたとは！ Love Childって題もいい．愛の夏の，愛の赤ちゃん(辞書にのってる「私生児」の意味は，結婚せずに子供を作るのがスキャンダラスだったころのもの)．この話を読むと，シャイアナはほんとうに，夢のシックスティーズの子供だったんだなあって思う．㊂

[3] Joseph: Maryの夫だったナザレの大工の名前
a fair assortment of Peters and Pauls: 「ピーター」や「ポール」をほどよく混ぜた，名前の取り合わせ．(ところで，Peter, Paul and Maryって聖人と聖母のバンドだったんですね．)

[4] a cross to bear: 「十字架を背負って歩く」という句が日本語にもあります．
Teachers would go out of their way to mispronounce it: 先生たちも(考えすぎて)わざわざ間違った発音をした

[6] it's phonetic!: スペル通りの読みでしょう！(たしかにShyは[ʃai], -anaは[ǽnə]としか読みようがない)
Montessori school: イタリアの教育家マリア・モンテッソリが提唱した教育法にもとづく「自由学園」．「私のころはボヘミアンの子が行ったけど，今はヤッピーの子が行くみたい」とはシャイアナの弁．

[7] roll sheet: クラスの名簿．「出席をとる」は "call the roll."

[9] "O": 『O嬢の物語』(*The Story of O*) から

[14] Summer of Love ... tie-dyed ... hand-made clothing: →注末の記事参照.

[17] graced the pages of the local paper: 地元の新聞に美しいヒッピーの親子の写真がのったわけ．アメリカの新聞は分厚く，何冊ものセクションに分かれている．シャイアナ一家の写真はそのうちのローカル・セクションにのったのだろう．第1面に目をひく写真と簡単な記事がのり，中のページに別の写真とより詳しい記事が続く——というのが報道のふつうの形で，だからここでもpagesと複数になっている．

[18] decked out in: ～で着飾った

[20] Scraps of velour [vəlúər] and silver lamé ... filled the quilt on my crib: 赤ちゃんベッドの掛け蒲団がベロア(ビロード系のふわふわ地)に銀ラメだなんて！

children of the 60's were supposed to be more open and enlightened than previous generations, but without totally insulting our parent's idealism, I have to say we were primarily considered "accessories."

We were taken everywhere — to bars and parties, to concerts [5] in Golden Gate Park and at the Fillmore Theater, and often even to work. I wish I could remember more of the concerts, since they earned a place in musical history, but all I can recall are moments of psychedelic light shows and snatches of songs. There are some recollections of the funky places we lived and even some [10] faces . . . Maria, who danced in a cage at night and sometimes baby-sat me during the day, and Carol and Renée (she was a flamenco dancer and he was an artist like my dad). There was also Gertrude Rosen, or "Git," who was one of my many godmothers and a godsend for my mother. Git was a school teacher [15] and she really influenced my mother as to the value of an education. Long before I was old enough for school, Git had me recognizing the alphabet and playing educational memory games. But, of course, it was *Sesame Street* that really taught me to read!

My parents were at an awkward age — much too young to be [20] of the Beat Generation, yet a few years older than most of the hippies. They were the first of their friends to have a child. As a result, I had many surrogate parents. Most of my parents friends were artists of sorts, and someone was always coming by with a new toy or puzzle they made or a piece of child-size furniture. I [25] remember loving the jigsaw puzzles, and had dozens of handmade ones, but my favorite was a store-bought puzzle with a Peter Max design . . . . I still have three pieces of it at my father's house in San Francisco.

My parents were born in the same city, Los Angeles, but their [30] childhoods took place on opposite ends of the economic spectrum. My mother's formative years found her sharing a one room shack with eight family members, raising chickens for the eggs that were almost the only protein in the Garcia diet. Meanwhile, in West L.A., my father shared eight course meals with one sib- [35]

[1] more open and enlightened： 社会慣習にとらわれず，未来の光や太古の叡智に導かれてより創造的に生きていく

[6] Golden Gate Park： ヘイト・アシュベリー地区の西側は，東西に長い公園になっている．67年の大々的なヒッピー集会をはじめ，あの時代，よくフリー・コンサートが開かれた．

Fillmore Theater： 中心街のマーケット通りとヴァネス通りの交叉点にあった，「ニューロックの殿堂」．同じくビル・グレアムの経営するニューヨークのホールとの対比でFillmore Westと呼ばれた．1971年閉鎖．「うちあげ」大コンサートを記録した『フィルモア最後の日』は，ロック・ドキュメンタリーの名作．

[10] funky places： 生活の臭いがぷんぷんした低所得者層の部屋．50年代のビート世代も，60年代のロック的感性も，こういう「おしゃれの反対」を愛したのだが，この「ファンキー」がポップ感覚の一つになって商業的に流通するのは70年代になってのこと．

[19] *Sesame Street*： 放送開始は1969年11月，シャイアナ2歳の時．

[20] awkward age： ふつうは10代なかばの年齢を指す言葉だ(った)けど，こういうふうに世代論にも使われる，というのはぼくも発見．ちなみにお父さんは1941年，お母さんは42年生まれ．

[24] artists of sorts： of sorts（なにかしらかの）がつくと，ちといかがわしい感じになる．何をやっているのかよくわからないけど，ヘンな，でも目は輝いているオジサンがしょっちゅうころがり込んできて，というようすをよく伝えている．

[27] Peter Max： 60年代にサイケデリック・ポスターでデビューしてから，たくさんのコマーシャルな企画で時代の風雲児となったポップ・デザイナー．

[31] opposite ends of the economic spectrum： アメリカは露骨な経済的階層社会．街はリッチな地区から貧しい地区へ，スペクトルをなして分離する．

[32] My mother's formative years found her sharing . . .： When she was growing up, my mother was sharing . . .

[34] almost the only protein in the Garcia diet： i.e., the Garcia family had scarcely any money to buy decent food.

[35] West L.A.： ダウンタウンの西側は，Beverly Hills, Santa Monica, Malibuなどを含む金のあふれる地区．これに対しEast Los Angeles地区はアフリカ系やメキシコ系住民であふれかえっている．

ling and a nanny. As I said, they were from different worlds.

However, they were both seeking something else; something "different." For my mother, that meant working to make her own money (but not until she paid off the only house her parents would ever own), and finding a better quality of life. For my fa- [5] ther, it also meant making his own money, while rejecting the obligations of an "heir." The quality of his life was not as much of a concern as the freedom to do "whatever the hell I want." This included getting expelled from practically every high school in the West Los Angeles school district, playing "extra" roles in the [10] worst "B-movies," a stint as an ambulance driver — which he still calls "a drag race with death" — and finally, running drugs up from Mexico. This last "job" finally brought him up to San Francisco, where the demand was greater than the already ample supply. [15]

My mother was already in San Francisco in 1965, living the life of an "office lady," when she met my dad at a New Year's party. In an era of "free love" their ensuing monogamy was considered quite an oddity. My father stopped going down to Mexico, my mother quit the insurance agency, and they started living to- [20] gether in a hotel in the North Beach area of San Francisco. I was conceived in the same hotel, within view of the flashing signs of "Big Al's" and "The Garden of Eden," just around the corner from City Lights Bookstore. My dad started "barking" in front of one of the strip joints across from their hotel to pay the rent, while [25] subsidizing their living expenses in less-than-legal ways.

They used his drug profits to buy silver beads and incredible fabrics. My father made necklaces and hats while my mother created costumes to fit the times. Bell-bottom hip-huggers in antique lace and stretch velour, decadent gowns of paisley velvet, and [30] fringed leather vests. She wore these outfits and was her own best advertisement. At 5′9″(175 cm) tall, with long black braids (before Cher!) and long brown legs — she definitely turned heads. They were extravagant fashions for people who had a flair for dressing up; the artists and poets, the strippers and musicians. Big Brother [35]

[8] "whatever the hell I want": the hell が入ることで「何やろうと俺の自由だ!」という激しい気持ちがこもってくる

[11] a stint: (職を転々とする状況で)ある仕事についていた時期

[12] "drag race with death": 救急車で飛ばすというのは「死が勝つか, 俺が勝つか」の路上レースをやるようなもの. 50年代, 60年代の不良っけのある少年たちの間で, 改造中古車 (hot rod) を使ってのスピードレースは大いに流行った.
running drugs up from Mexico: この時代の映画『イージー・ライダー』も, メキシコからドラッグを運んで金をつくるところで始まっている.

[17] "office lady": シャイアナが日本で知った和製英語.

[18] their ensuing monogamy: そういえば, ぼくの周りには, ラディカルな顔をして, しっちゃかめっちゃかな生活をしているくせに, 長く連れ合う夫婦が多い. この本の著者たちも, Jerry も Larry もそろそろ銀婚式って感じだし(おっとわが家もか), Dan はその遥か上をいっている. Paul もセカンド・マリッジは順調だし . . . あれれ, 何を書いているんだぁ?

[21] a hotel in the North Beach area: ホテルといっても, この辺には古くていかがわしいのが多い.

[23] "Big Al's" and "The Garden of Eden": Broadway と Columbus Avenue が交叉する North Beach のこのあたりは, ニューヨークの42番街, 新宿歌舞伎町に相当する歓楽街. ヌードの踊り子を見ながら酒を飲む strip joints がいっぱいある.

[24] City Lights Bookstore: この歓楽街にある, ビート文学のメッカ. 今も文学関係の品揃えは最高. コーヒーの飲める地下のフロアにはホモセクシュアルの集会など無数の文化的催しのビラが置かれている.
"barking": 客引きをやってたわけ.

[26] subsidizing: 正規の雇用以外の方法で生活資金を得るときに使う. *I'm working part-time at Shakey's Pizza, but I'm subsidizing my college expenses by selling crack.*

[29] Bell-bottom hip-huggers: 太くて高いヒールの靴にベルボトムといういでたちはこのごろ東京でもたまに見かけるけれど, ベルトが骨盤の下にくるほど股上の短いヒップハガー・タイプのジーンズはどこにいったの?

[30] stretch velour: ベルベットの肌ざわりで伸縮する, うっとりするような生地.

[31] wore these outfits and was her own best advertisement: 彼女の服装が, 最高に魅力的な自分を演出した, ということ.

[33] Cher: 歌手で女優のシェールがいくつにも編んだ髪を垂らし, その上からヘッドバンドを巻いてインディアンのイメージを強調していたのは, 1976–77年にかけてのテレビ番組 "The Sonny and Cher Show" でのこと.

and the Holding Company crashed in the same Broadway hotel, and my mother dressed Janis Joplin many times. One of my mother's favorite memories is of Joplin, voice soaked in Southern Comfort, singing verses of "Summertime" to me at a fitting. Too bad the clothes outlived many of the characters. [5]

Luckily for me, my mother liked being in control too much to really get sucked into the drug scene. Growing up in the worst part of East L.A., watching her sisters and their gangs terrorize each other, had made life a little too valuable to be wasted. My dad did it all, in abundance, but in the end he survived because he [10] never lost sight of this maxim: "drugs are for profit." He made it through the 1960's and the 1970's intact, having a brief setback in the 1980's with a drug-induced stroke, but he pulled through that with a record-breaking recovery. For his fiftieth birthday, he bought himself a new Kawasaki racing motorcycle, and I'm sure [15] he's riding as I'm writing.

Now for the story of my name. My name came to them in the middle of North Beach when my mom was eight months pregnant. Actually, my name was bestowed upon them on a crowded public bus, by my father's ex-girlfriend. Her name was Shirley [20] Wahoo, and I don't know if it was truly an ancestral name, but everyone said she was Eskimo. They also said she was into black magic and curses, so when she came up to them on the bus and placed her hands on my mother's bulging stomach, my mom was less than pleased. But Shirley Wahoo just said "Her name will be [25] Shyana" and moved to the back of the bus. Until that moment, my parents had chosen not to know the sex of their baby but, after she calmed down, my mom went home and made my first dress. They never discussed naming me anything different, but they did have a friend call Shirley Wahoo to check the spelling and mean- [30] ing. Apparently, it is also Eskimo and, loosely translated, it means "woman who walks in the dark" . . . or so said Shirley Wahoo. I've never found it in any book, poem, or song, although there is a god named "Shyama" in the Hindu *Mahabharata*.

There were times when the taunts of other children made me [35]

[35] Big Brother and the Holding Company : ヘイト・アシュベリー(次頁の補注参照)で結成された生粋のカウンターカルチャー・バンド．ジャニスの加入後一躍メジャーに踊りでた．

[1] crashed : 押しかけてきた

[3] voice soaked in Southern Comfort, singing verses of "Summertime" : 酒飲みの南部女ジャニスが，バーボンをベースにしたリキュールをあおって，南部の田舎の情景が詰まった子守歌を歌う，涙が出てきそうな情景．"Summertime" の熱唱は，「ジョップリン・イン・コンサート」に収められているのがベストだと思います．

[4] fitting : 衣装の寸法合わせ

Too bad the clothes outlived many of the characters : ドレスは残り，ジャニスはもういない．ジム・モリソンもジミ・ヘンドリックスもいない . . .

[7] get sucked into the drug scene : ドラッグに溺れてボロボロになっていく．ジャニスの伝記映画『ローズ』で，ベット・ミドラーが演じたみたいになっていくこと．

[9] My dad did it all, in abundance : そっちの方は父親がふんだんにやっていた

[11] made it through the 1960's and 1970's intact : survived those years without getting seriously hurt

[12] having a brief setback . . . with a drug-induced stroke : ドラッグが原因の発作によって短期間，活動停止状態になる

[13] pull(ed) through : 切り抜ける

[22] into black magic and curses : 当時フィルモアのレギュラーだったサンタナの後の大ヒットに「ブラック・マジック・ウーマン」というのがあった．

[25] less than pleased : not quite pleased. 次の "after she calmed down" というところからもわかるように，本当は really upset したわけだけど，そういうときにストレートじゃない表現をして味を出す話法は，英語でも発達しています．

[29] did have a friend call Shirley Wahoo : 友達に頼んでシャーリー・ワフーに電話してもらった

[32] . . . or so said Shirley Wahoo : 少なくともシャーリーはそう言った

hate my name, made me wish it was "normal." My mother likes to tell the story of me coming home from school one day to announce: "I'm not 'shy' anymore, so now you can just call me 'Anna'!" After she explained it wasn't an adjective describing my personality, I was crestfallen. But over time, I've grown to appreciate its uniqueness . . . and even to like it. Even its meaning seems appropriate to me, since I am definitely a nocturnal person. Besides, I was lucky; they could have named me something really bizarre like "Moonflower."

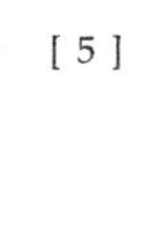

Baby Shyana

[5] crestfallen : それまでの威勢の良さがふっとんだようす
over time : やがて；時が経るうちに

若い読者への補注：「花のサンフランシスコ」

■

"Summer of Love" といえば1967年．ところはサンフランシスコ．Height通りとAshbury通り一帯には，全米から集まったflower childrenが群れていた．彼らは**tie-dyed shirt** (psychedelicな絞り染め)を着，目の荒いレース編み (**macramé**)や，かぎ針編み (**crochet** [krouʃéi]) のドレスでゆったり体を包み，顔にハートやピース・マークをペイントし，髪に花をかざし，マリワナの煙を吸い込み，ブルージーなロックに心をあずけ，宇宙との交感を夢見た．メディアも彼らに好意的だった．宇宙衛星でthe Beatlesが"All You Need Is Love"を歌ったこの夏，ラブとピースとフラワーは，革命後の未来へのパスポートのように思えた．

その20年前には，後に**Beat Generation**と呼ばれる若者たちが，市の北東部，波止場近くのNorth Beach界隈で詩とジャズに高揚したボヘミアン的生活を営んでいた．50年代後半，Allen Ginsberg, Jack Kerouacらの詩と小説が出版されると，彼らの夢幻的な陶酔感覚は，熱狂的な追従者を生み出した．65年末あたりからざわめき始めたcountercultureは，このビート文化が大衆化していったものだといえる．メディアによって**hippies**と呼ばれた彼らは，squareで気持ち悪い仕事社会から切れて，愛と気持ちよさに導かれた**hand-made**の現実を自分の手でクリエートすることに精進した．そんな彼らにとって，JimとかJaneとかいう伝統的な名前はなにか古くて醜い世界に自分を縛り付けておく絆みたいに感じられた．で，自分たちの赤ちゃんには，なにかもっとbeautifulな名前を――というわけで，RainbowとかRiver (Phoenix君，安らかに)とか，派手な名前をもつ子供たちが一部の地域で量産されたわけである．

Summer of Loveのナイーブな輝きは2年ともたなかった．シックスティーズは混迷化し，たくさんの人生を押しつぶす結果になった．あの時代がファッションになって軽々しく戻ってきたのは80年代末から．今Height-AshburyやBerkeleyのTelegraph Avenueの露店では，強烈な模様のtie-dyed shirtsがふんだんに売られている．色と図柄は残り，「意味」は風化する．なつかしの反体制ファッションは，同じ時代，テレビのポップス番組を彩っていた**white vinyl go-go boots** (ウゴウゴ・ルーガ，じゃなくてゴーゴー・ガールがミニスカートと一緒に必ずはいていた)と，いまじゃどこも変わらない．

SESSION 3

Flea Market Metaphysics

■

Leza Lowitz

THE FIRST TIME I went to the flea market was in America's bicentennial year of 1976. One Sunday morning my favorite aunt, Peggy, picked me up in her orange VW van and drove me out to the drive-in theater near the Alameda Naval Base. Peggy was a social worker who drove an orange VW van with small [5] windows on the tops and sides that made it seem like a movable greenhouse. She wore patchouli oil and huaraches and had boyfriends from all over the world. On the way I asked her if she wanted some bubblegum and she said no, that her jaw was tired. She said it was like the way the hand got tired holding a pen [10] when writing. I'd never even conceived of the possibility that the jaw could be tired. It was the first of many revelations that were to come to me at the flea market.

I was an utterly nihilistic teenager, my head full of radioactive warnings and doomsday scenarios of an all-out nuclear war (I [15] prayed for the epicenter). Nothing impressed me. Nothing even moved me, but somehow, I felt at home at the flea market, where things had chips and imperfections, where they smelled of dust and rust and mold and life. It was a place, I realized, unafraid of death in a time the country was wholeheartedly celebrating its [20] sanitized-for-television "birth."

リザ・ローウィッツはアメリカ西海岸に育った詩人・小説家．詩集に *old ways to fold / New Paper* などがある．1990 年から 94 年，日本に住み，日本女性の詩・俳句・短歌の翻訳もしていて (*A long rainy season*, Stone Bridge Press, 1994 など)，東京大学で教えたこともある．現在は東京で，創作に携わりながらヨガ教室を経営している．ホームページは http://www.lezalowitz.com. ⓛ

[2] bicentennial year： 200 周年

[3] VW： Volkswagen

[4] the Alameda Naval Base： カリフォルニア州，オークランド市に接する海軍の大航空基地．

[7] patchouli [pǽtʃuli] oil： インド・ビルマ産の木から作るオイル．次の huaraches とともに，自由で型にはまらないライフスタイルを感じさせる．

huaraches： [wərɑ́ːtʃiːz] かかとの低い，上部が編み革のサンダル．ビーチ・ボーイズの「サーフィン U.S.A.」の歌い出しにも，"If everybody had an ocean across the U.S.A. / Then everybody'd be surfin' like Ca-li-for-ni-a / You'd see 'em wearin' their baggies, huarache sandals too"（もしもアメリカじゅう海があったら / みんなキャ・ライ・フォ・ナイ・エイみたいにサーフィンするさ / 短パンはいて，ワラチサンダルはいて）とある．

[14] nihilistic： 意味は「ニヒリスティック」でよいが読み方は [náiəlìstik].

radioactive warnings： 放射性汚染に関する警告

[15] doomsday scenario(s)： 「この世の終わりのシナリオ」．湾岸戦争あたりから，日本語でも，戦争の予測などに「シナリオ」という言葉が使われるようになってきた．

all-out： total

I prayed for the epicenter： epicenter は「震央」の意もあるが，ここは核の落ちる「爆心」．放射能の後遺症に苦しんで生きのびるより，あっさり死んでしまう方がましだと思ったということ．

[18] chips： 欠け目，傷

dust and rust and mold and life： 4 つ並んだ名詞のうち，英語では dust and rust の部分が韻を踏んでいるが，訳すと rust and mold の部分（錆びとカビ）の部分が韻を踏む．どうでもいいことですが．

[20] its sanitized-for-television "birth"： テレビ向けに消毒・殺菌した「誕生」．消毒された 200 年祭が流通するそうした流れのなかから振り落とされた，死を恐れぬ (unafraid of death) 生活の臭い（19 行の life）が，フリーマーケットでは堂々と息づいている．

The flea market was a place where people engaged in the nine-
teenth-century pastime of collecting objects with the twentieth-
century caveat that the things were worthless, to be collected for
some imaginary future time when they might be "worth something." These were not coins or stamps in limited editions or spe- [5]
cial mints, nor butterflies proven rare and precious. What you
found: boxes of buttons, old tools, beads, license plates, cowboy
boots, Fiestaware or Bakelite jewelry. To enter those booths was
to enter small worlds made up of the detritus of the modern
world, T. S. Eliot's "fragments shored against our ruins." Each [10]
booth was like a different slide in a magic lantern show,
someone's personal universe in disarray. Up for Sale. No questions asked.

People arrived before dawn, their cars loaded down and roped
up with belongings like a scene from *Tobacco Road*. Sometimes [15]
they didn't even have a chance to unpack their boxes, since the
other vendors would start to rummage through them to get the
best deals, which they'd turn around and sell that very day. I
went there every Sunday while my friends spent their Sundays
wandering the mall. [20]

I never liked the mall. For one thing, I'd never seen an antique
store in a mall. On the other hand, I got annoyed when vendors
opened stalls at the flea market displaying products still in their
shrink-wrapped casings, because new things didn't belong at the
flea market. [25]

We go to the mall because it insulates us from life. We go to the
flea market to embrace the ghost of a scavenger past we've sold
out in favor of malls and bicentennial celebrations. We think of
friends we've had, lovers we've lost, times irretrievable, but
things show up at the flea market and *make us remember* [30]
times, places and people we didn't even know we forgot. New
things have no history, no frame of reference; they're just prod-

[3] caveat: warning; caution
[5] in limited editions or special mints: 限定版，特別鋳造の
[7] license plates: 自動車のナンバープレート
[8] Fiestaware: フィエスタ焼き．1936年から作られはじめ，コスト高などの理由で70年代初頭に製造中止になったが，いまだ愛好者は多く，各種各色を揃えようとするマニアのあいだで高値を呼んだりもする．インターネットにも "the Internet's Fiestaware Forum" がある．
[9] detritus: 岩などが壊れた破片
[10] T. S. Eliot's "fragments shored against our ruins": T・S・エリオットの有名な詩「荒地」(The Waste Land) の結末の "These fragments I have shored against my ruins"（こうした言葉の断片で私は身の破滅を防いできた）を踏まえた言い方．「荒地」は1922年に発表された，その後の現代詩におそらくもっとも大きな影響を与えた作品．文明を廃墟と捉える姿勢は，1920年代には一種の知的ファッションだった．
[11] magic lantern: 旧式の幻燈機
[12] in disarray: 混沌とした
Up for Sale: 売りに出ている
[14] load(ed) down: (荷物を)ぎっしり積み込む
[15] *Tobacco Road*: アースキン・コールドウェルの，アメリカ南部の貧農の生活を描いた小説(1932)．1941年，ジョン・フォードが映画化．
[17] vendors: sellers
rummage: ひっかき回す
[18] turn around: 「向きを変える」とは，いま買ったばかりの物を，今度は売り物にするということ．
[20] the mall: 町外れにゆったりとしたスペースをとったショッピング・モールは，都市内奥部にとり残された貧しい人々のバザールの場フリーマーケットとは好対照．
[23] stalls: 屋台
[24] shrink-wrapped casings: ぴっちりしたビニール包装
[26] insulate(s): 絶縁する，防護する
[27] scavenger past: (ハイエナのように)どんなものでもあさりまくった過去の時代
sold out in favor of malls: モールと引き換えに売り渡してしまった．sell out には，主義を捨てて何か大切なものを手放してしまう，というニュアンスが伴う．*He used to be a good singer, but he* sold out *and now just sings for money.*
[29] irretrievable: 取り返しのつかない
[32] frame of reference: よりどころとなる枠組

ucts. Most of the time, I go to the flea market not to buy anything, but to be reminded of a past just distant enough to make it seem imagined. Remember those? We ask our companions, looking at an old sewing machine in a wooden desk, or a manual egg beater/ceramic bowl contraption. Didn't Mom use to have one [5] just like that in the days before Cuisinarts? Whatever happened to it?

I never saw any fleas at the flea market.

According to the dictionary, they were members of one of the 1,600 species and subspecies of small, wingless, blood-sucking [10] insects of the order *siphonaptera*, small vampires that bit into the skin, moving from host to host transmitting disease. To me, fleas were little black dots that multiplied soundlessly and invisibly in the hidden universe of places like my dog's coat. In fact, I'd only seen them floating dead in the bathwater after I'd washed my [15] black Labrador, Minnie Babe. I came to respect them when I learned that they had powerful leg muscles that enabled them to jump distances up to 200 times their body length at an acceleration of more than 200 cm/s^2. This amazing strength enabled them to pull miniature cars and perform other stunts in "Flea Cir- [20] cuses." The idea appealed to me, because if the flea market was a circus of sorts, where freaks and outcasts and mystics could belong, then an alienated teenager could find a home there, too.

Imagining that this was where the name came from, I was disappointed to find out that the first flea market in Paris in 1922 was [25] called the Marché aux Puces because the second-hand articles were so old and decrepit they were believed to gather fleas. Still, people often mistook the name for "free market" — not because it was a loophole for free enterprise, a bit like cheating the system (which it was), but because things were so cheap there as to be [30] almost free.

[4] egg beater: 泡立て器

[5] contraption: (妙に凝った)機械

Didn't Mom use to . . .: used to ～の(否定の)疑問形.「～しなかったっけ?」.

[6] Cuisinarts: クイジナート社製のフードプロセッサー. 1970年代前半からアメリカで売られはじめ, 70年代後半から家庭に浸透.

[8] I never saw any fleas at the flea market: 後出のように, flea market という言い方はフランス語 marché aux puces (puce は蚤) に由来する.

[10] species and subspecies: 種と, (それよりさらに細かい)亜種

[11] order: 目(もく). 動物は class, order, family, genus, species(, subspecies), variety という順序で分類される.

[12] host: (寄生動植物の)寄主

[14] coat: 動物の毛皮・毛のこと.

[18] acceleration: 加速度

[20] stunts: 離れ業.「スタントマン」のスタントに同じ.

[21] a circus of sorts: サーカスといえなくもないもの

[22] freaks and outcasts and mystics: 畸型の人間や, 世のなかからこぼれ落ちた人間や, 神秘家

[23] alienated: 世の中からずれた

[27] decrepit: in bad condition

[28] people often mistook the name for "free market": L と R の区別がつかない日本人にはなおさら.

[29] loophole for free enterprise: 個人が何の制約も受けず自由に商売できるという意味での「自由企業制度の抜け道」

a bit like: a little like

[30] which it was: 事実その通りだった(事実「体制」を欺くものだった)

Call it what you will, unlike a mall, a flea market was nomadic.
It was portable. It could be anywhere — a bird market in a Paris
métro, a Shinto shrine in Tokyo, a Zen temple in Kyoto, or a
drive-in theater in Alameda County, California. The flea market
was the closest thing America had to the European *marktplatz* or [5]
the Arab *souk*. First there were the smells — of Chinese jasmine or
Indian sandalwood incense mingled with the bitter vapors of
home-cooked hamhocks, chitlins and greens from the Soul Food
Kitchen, or the heavy spice of chili oil from the chop suey and egg
rolls fried up in the Lotus Garden trailer's rusted iron woks. Then, [10]
there was the fact that you could sell anything, or buy anything,
too.

If you were like me, you came as much for the seller as for the
goods. I met actors between roles, students saving money for college, people selling just to engage in their passion for collecting — [15]
like the man who sold rows of reconditioned cowboy boots in lizard, crocodile and plain old leather. He could well have been a
blanket trader in a covered wagon in *The Wild, Wild West*, and his
prices were so high it seemed as if he didn't want to sell anything.
My favorite seller was a black man with nappy grey hair who sold [20]
boxes of buttons, beads and watch parts all mixed together. He
said "arigatoo gozaimasu" in perfect Japanese and told me of
fighting in Okinawa. He sold me a plastic Jesus but believed in
the Buddha. There were hippies in their converted vans selling
trinkets from Bali, men from Africa selling beads and baskets, [25]
Korean families selling rows of neatly folded socks and boxes of
beauty amenities, many languages floating in the air. The flea
market was the place where the "other" — the exotic, eccentric,
the marginal — found a place. Things that fell through the cracks
fell there. How did they get there? How did we get there? It [30]
makes us ask.

Philosopher, gambler, poet, martyr, they were all there, haggling and bantering. The vendors didn't care how long it took to

[1] Call it what you will: それをどう呼ぼうとも
nomadic: 遊牧の

[3] métro: 地下鉄
Shinto shrine: 神社

[4] Alameda County: オークランド市を含む，サンフランシスコ湾東岸の一地域.

[5] *marktplatz*: 市の立つ広場(ドイツ語).

[6] *souk*: [suːk] アラビア語で「市」「バザール」の意.

[7] sandalwood: 白檀(ビャクダン). 香気があり，香(incense)などに用いられる.
mingled with: 〜と混ざりあって
vapors: 湯気

[8] hamhocks: 豚の足肉
chitlins: 小腸. hamhocks 同様，アメリカ南部の黒人にとっての「郷愁」の味.
greens: 青菜
the Soul Food Kitchen: いかにも黒人が経営していそうな屋台名. soul food は アメリカ南部の黒人の伝統的な食べ物. soul music, soul brother (黒人仲間) など，"soul" という言葉には，黒人たちの自文化への誇りがこもる.

[9] chop suey: 八宝菜に近いアメリカ式中国料理.
egg rolls: 春巻. これもアメリカでポピュラー.

[10] the Lotus Garden: いかにも中国人が経営していそう.
woks: 中華鍋

[14] actors between roles: ひとつの役を終えて次の役を待っている(要するに当面仕事のない)役者

[16] reconditioned: 修理済みの
lizard, crocodile: トカゲ，ワニ

[17] could well have been . . .: 〜だったとしても全然不思議はなかった

[18] *The Wild, Wild West*: スパイ物の発想を取り入れたテレビ西部劇(1965–70).

[20] nappy: 縮れた

[24] converted: 改造した

[25] trinkets: 安手の小物

[27] beauty amenities: 化粧品の小物

[28] the "other": 他者

[29] Things that fell through the cracks: 社会のひび割れたすきまからこぼれ落ちたものたち

[32] martyr: [máːrtər] 殉教者
haggling: haggle は「値切る」

[33] banter(ing): (悪意なく)からかう，ひやかす

make a sale — they were in there for the duration. Happy to arrive early and stay late, no tyranny of the timeclock to watch over them, nor boss to dismiss them. Just open your card table and lay your wares on it. There's no catalogue at the flea market. No mail order. No back order, either. Just the present in a world of past [5] objects. I can still remember the first thing I ever bought there — a pair of antique sterling silver rings made in Siam, commissioned by a traveling American explorer (or was he a salesman?) for his newlywed wife. The couple had been married over fifty years and it was the occasion of her death that finally got the rings off her [10] fingers. The vendor had bought them at an estate sale, and I bought them as much for the story as for the rings themselves — not knowing or even caring if it was true. One is a solid silver dome, the other is a woven knot. I wear them religiously. The first time I saw them they seemed to hold secrets of a far-off world: [15] where was Siam anyway, and how did one get there in the 1920's, and who called it that anymore?

Of all the things I loved about the place, what I loved best was the fact that you got dirty. By the time you were ready to leave, your pants were covered in mud and you were inevitably wear- [20] ing a mantle of dust. Add that to the fact that you had to use an outhouse, and you were grateful for it, too. How many places are there where you can get dirty shopping, or think about the jaw being tired? To me, going to the flea market was a little like playing jacks in the age of Nintendo. Low tech. Up to chance. Close to [25] the ground. Subject to dirt and rust.

When Steve Erickson was once asked to write about the "spiritual center" of Los Angeles, he wrote of a place called the Star Strip. Despite the celestial leanings its name might suggest, it's a strip joint on La Ciénega Boulevard. If I'd been asked to nominate [30] the "spiritual center" of the San Francisco Bay Area, you can guess what I would say. The competition is stiff, too, this being the birthplace of new "religions" such as est — not to mention the

[1] they were in there for the duration : 「どうせずっとそこにいるのだから」. 単に「一日中」というだけでなく, 生き方としてそこにいることを選んでいる, というニュアンスが感じられる.

[2] no tyranny of the timeclock to watch over them : 彼らを監視するタイムレコーダーの専制もなく

[3] card table : トランプ用テーブル. 折りたたみ式の真四角の小さなテーブル. 蚤の市で店を開くにはこれで十分.

[4] wares : 売り物

[5] back order : 繰越し注文. 在庫がないときに, とりあえず注文だけ受けて, 品が入り次第発送すること.

[7] sterling silver : スターリング銀(銀含有率 92.5% 以上の法定純銀)

Siam : [saiǽm] タイの旧名.

commission(ed) : 製作を依頼する, 注文する

[11] estate sale : 金持ちが死んだあとに行なわれる, 遺品売り立て

[13] a solid silver dome : ドーム型に盛り上がった銀の塊.

[14] woven knot : 針金状の銀を編み込んだ格好をした指輪.

[17] who called it that anymore? : that は Siam を指す. いまでは誰もが Thailand と呼ぶ.

[21] mantle : マント, 外套

[22] outhouse : 戸外便所

[23] the jaw being tired : アゴが疲れるのは, むろん喋りまくるため.

[25] jacks : 六角の金属の小片で遊ぶ, おはじきに似たゲーム.

Up to chance : 運任せ

Close to the ground : 「地面に近い」というのは, 確固としたものに根差している感じ.

[26] Subject to dirt and rust : 泥汚れ・錆あり

[27] Steve Erickson : 本書第 5 章の筆者でもある, ロサンゼルス在住の作家.

[29] celestial leanings : 天国を思わせる雰囲気

[30] strip joint : ストリップ酒場

La Ciénega Boulevard : ロサンゼルス中心街を南北に貫く大通り.

[31] the San Francisco Bay Area : サンフランシスコ, オークランド, サンノゼ等を含む, ロサンゼルスに次ぐカリフォルニアの大都市圏.

[32] stiff : きびしい

[33] est : Werner Erhard が 1971 年にはじめた自己発見・実現システム. 一種の新興宗教.

strip joints on Broadway, which some might (and apparently do) consider serious contenders.

That's why on Sunday mornings you'll find me not in the church or synagogue, but slowly walking the labyrinth of the dusty world of this nuclear mall. Not looking to buy anything in [5] particular, I'm full of the grace of wanting something to happen. To me, the repetition of the not-quite-square booths is as comforting as a prayer or a sutra — each one holding the promise of a new discovery or revelation. And isn't that what religion is all about anyway? [10]

Postscript:

Despite a decade-long effort by customers, vendors, local activists and heroes to keep it going, this year the Marin City Flea Market, one of the last flea markets in Northern California, was torn down and replaced by a shopping mall with ample parking. [15] "Don't it always seem to go / That you don't know what you've got / Till it's gone / They paved paradise / And put up a parking lot." — Joni Mitchell, "Big Yellow Taxi"

[1] Broadway： 第2章の筆者シャイアナ・クアシャの生まれたホテルがあったあたりの目抜き通り．

[2] contender(s)： ライバル，候補者

[4] synagogue： ユダヤ教会
labyrinth： 迷宮

[5] nuclear mall： 「蚤の市」の言い換え．この nuclear は，nuclear family(核家族)を連想させると同時に，「核の時代」にも生き残るしたたかさを暗示している．そう言えばスティーヴ・エリクソンも，核の時代の想像力を "nuclear imagination" と呼んだ．
looking to： planning to; expecting to

[6] full of the grace of wanting something to happen： 「何かが起こって欲しいという気持ちに胸をふくらませている」．grace には「神の恩寵」の意味があり，ここでもそうした宗教的ニュアンスが残っている．

[8] sutra： 仏教の経

[9] isn't that what religion is all about： 「宗教って要するにそういうものじゃないだろうか」．that は the promise of a new discovery or revelation を指す．

SESSION 4

Motherland

■

Paul Alkebulan

> "I was born by the river in a little tent and just like the river I've been running ever since. It's been a long time coming but I know my change is going to come." Sam Cooke

I MUST BE GETTING old. My son just started driving the family car and this week he's bringing his girlfriend over for Thanksgiving dinner. It seems like only yesterday that I was showing him how to cross the street and giving him a child's dictionary to read for bedtime. The news just came on about the [5] death of Cab Calloway. My son Bomani shook hands with him once at UC Berkeley. We were there for a screening of the Blues Brothers movie starring Calloway, Dan Aykroyd, and John Belushi. I wanted my son to meet the great man (Mr. Hi-de-ho himself). It was important to me for him to connect with our cul- [10] tural past and to have some sense of where we came from. He always remembered his encounter with Calloway and I was pleased that I had arranged it. Now Calloway is gone and my 18 year old son will be able to say that he once met his eminence. I'm getting a lot of pleasure out of watching him and his friends grow [15] up and start their lives.

Most of them are attending college either locally or out of state. They appear to be doing OK as these things are measured at this stage of their lives. Bomani is studying graphic arts at Laney College and working as an Instructional Aide with the local school [20] district. He wants to transfer to UC when he finishes at Laney. His girlfriend is working at a pet store and wants to be a veterinarian.

1981年バークレイの大学に移ったとき，住むのはファンキーな場所にしたいと思って，数マイル南のオークランド市，グローブ・ストリートのアパートに住んだ．この地域(40丁目)の住人は多くがアフリカ系かメキシコ系で，同じアパートのはす向かいに住んでいたのがポールだった．週末になると，離婚した妻のもとから5歳のボマニがやってくる．彼の部屋からはいつも，ボブ・マーリーのレゲエ音楽と，テレビニュースを見ながらレーガンを罵る声と，落ち込んだときにかけるというマルコムXの演説レコードが聞こえてきていた．黒人文化についてのぼくの教師であるポールの日本登場は『マルコムXワールド』(径書房) に続いて2度目．現在バージニア州立大学歴史学助教授．㋚

Sam Cooke: ゴスペル・シンガーからポピュラー界に登場したソウル・ミュージックのパイオニア．1957年暮れに「ユー・センド・ミー」の大ヒットを放つ．

[3] Thanksgiving dinner: 遠くに暮らしている家族もみんな集まって，七面鳥のディナーを食べる11月の第4木曜日はアメリカの国民の休日．

[6] Cab Calloway: ダボダボの「ズートスーツ」を着て，派手なしぐさでジャズ・ナンバーを歌いまくった．「ミニー・ザ・ムーチャー」が1933年に大ヒット．歌詩を忘れると "Hi-de-ho, hi-de-hi-hi" とかスキャットして，それでまた人気が出た．1994年，87歳で死去．

Bomani: 口絵写真でぼくの膝にのっている．ヒッピーたちが自分の子供にどんな名前をつけたかは Shyana のエッセイに面白く書かれているけれど，黒人ナショナリストは自分の子供に，どこかアフリカの民族の言葉を選んでつけた．ポールによれば，ボマニ(アメリカ発音は「バモニ」に近い)はどこかの(聞いたが忘れた)部族の「戦士」の意味．実はポールの姓ももともとは Fleming だったが，白人姓を嫌って今のに変えた．

[7] UC: University of California. バークレーの他，UCLA, UCSD (San Diego), UC Davis など，いくつかの別個の州立大学の総称．

the Blues Brothers: テレビの人気ドタバタ番組 *Saturday Night Live* のコメディアン，ダン・アクロイドと故ジョン・ベルーシの役柄．彼らを主役にした1980年の映画 (邦題「ブルース・ブラザース」) には，キャロウェイ，レイ・チャールズ，アリサ・フランクリンといった黒人アーティストの大物が次つぎ登場する．

[14] his eminence: 聖人・偉人に対し，単に he, him という代わりに用いる．

[18] as these things are measured at this stage of their lives: 18歳という年から判断してみれば

[20] Instructional Aide: 小学校で先生のアシスタントをするお兄さん，お姉さん

[21] transfer to UC: Dan McLeod の入学試験の説明(122ページ，33行)参照

It seems that this generation is off on their own journey of discovery. As they work their way thru life they will encounter some of the same difficulties that we did but many things will be different. They'll have to possess more technical skills than we ever did. Their knowledge of racism will have to be very sophisticated and [5] this will demand that they have a profound understanding of the history of Africa and her descendants all over the world. Fortunately, as a history teacher I can help them in this regard.

Throughout my adult life I have tried to cultivate ties with blacks from all over the world. We are very fortunate that we live [10] in a place that serves as a nexus for different cultures and people. This gives them a good start on participating in this global village of ours. I recently fulfilled a lifelong goal of mine by visiting Africa. I should have gone before but I console myself by noting that events occur in their appointed time. The African people are very [15] hardworking and survival-oriented. The infrastructure is not as strong as it could or should be. But I'm used to hardship so that wasn't really important to me. My childhood years in the South prepared me for some of the obstacles.

In Motherland I saw and learned what I wanted to. It was clear [20] to me that many of the cultural habits and speech patterns that we use in this country are a direct descendant of our West African past. They've managed to survive over hundreds of years in a very modified form. I attribute this to a variety of factors, but I believe the most important is this: up until 30 or so years ago we [25] lived in fairly self-contained communities where it was much easier to transmit the values that were important to us and had meaning within our own social context. These values and cultural patterns are African-centered and managed to keep us alive in America for centuries. At their heart is a recognition that we are [30] strangers in a strange land and in order to survive we need to maintain our own cultural identity. Any adaptions have to be as suitable to us as possible under the circumstances. Social integration had its positive aspects but it certainly tore a hole in our cultural fabric. The negative results are being felt as we speak. [35]

[1] off on their own journey : 自分たちの世代が通ってきたのとは違った道を歩いている

[2] work their way thru life : 人生をがんばって歩んでいく

[5] Their knowledge of racism will have to be very sophisticated : 60年代初頭には，白人と同じレストランで食事できたり，同じ大学に入れたりすることが，racism との闘いの目標だった．たてまえ上は人種的平等が確立し，テレビ局がキャスターなどにも有色人種を使うことに異様なほど過敏になっている今日，人種差別はより目に見えにくいものとなって続いている．

[9] to cultivate ties with blacks from all over the world : マルコム X は最終的に「万国の黒人の連帯」を訴える立場にたったが，それは現在も民族意識の高い黒人たちに継承されている．オークランドでも，しばしば西アフリカや西インド諸島との民間交流の場がもたれる．ポールはそうした企画に今も積極的だ．

[11] serves as a nexus : ネットワークの中心として機能する．ニューヨークのハーレムやシカゴのサウスサイドに続き，オークランドは常に西海岸の黒人文化活動の本拠地としての役割をはたしてきた．

[12] gives them a good start on : prepares them well for

[15] events occur in their appointed time : 物事は運命の定める時がきてはじめて起こるものだ

[16] infrastructure : 鉄道，道路，学校，病院など，生活や産業の基盤となる部分

[18] My childhood years in the South . . . the obstacles : アメリカは衛生状態の悪いスラムであっても，給湯・電話・交通等，生活面での便利さは整っているが，ポールが育った50年代のバージニアの田舎は，もっと第三世界的だったのだろう．

[23] survive over hundreds of years : 17世紀も半ばになると北米大陸の各植民地で次々と奴隷制度が合法化され，たくさんの奴隷船が到着するようになった．

[26] self-contained communities : 外部に頼らず生活を成り立たせている共同体

[29] . . . are African-centered and managed to keep us alive in America : 白人の価値観にからめとられてしまったら，我々のアフリカ人としての生活は破壊されてしまっただろう，という考えを背景にした表現．

[31] strangers in a strange land : 60年代にカルト的人気を誇ったハインラインのSF小説のタイトルが，*Stranger in a Strange Land*.

[32] Any adaptions have to be suitable to us : アメリカという場所に適応するとしても，それはアフリカ人である我々に適した形でなければならない

[33] Social integration : 白人たちと社会的に統合融和していくこと．キング牧師ら穏健派の運動家の立場だった．

It's funny how life boils down to the simple things when all is said and done. I've spent most of my life as an activist, challenging the established order of white supremacy and working for the liberation of African people. When I was younger I was a member of Black Panther Party. We were guided by what we called our [5] 10-point program and platform. This was our organizational and ideological guideline. We wanted freedom and the ability to determine our own destiny. In order to achieve this power we wanted to awaken our people to their latent and actual human potential to become fully productive and self-actualized people. [10] In order to wake folks up, we embarked on a nationwide organizing campaign to address some of the pressing needs of our communities: housing, education, health, police brutality, jobs, etc. This campaign threatened the power structure because we related to our own heroes like Malcolm X rather than manufactured [15] negroes who were placed in front of us in order to pacify the community. Our determination to make a change was unshakable. We were defeated because the government was stronger, not because they were more just. When we look back on that period, I'm proud of the fight that we made and the way we did it. We identi- [20] fied the problem and confronted it in a direct manly fashion just as Malcolm would have wanted us to do it.

As time has moved on it's very clear that any effective program starts at home and spreads out from there. The established order depends on disorganization, demoralization, disunity and de- [25] featism. It demands that people act as individuals instead of a unit. Materialism is stressed over spiritual values. These negative tendencies can be overcome by stressing the family-centered values that enabled Africans to survive in this land. This can only be taught at home and is the only viable answer to the urban nihil- [30] ism that surrounds us.

Young people in this community are presented with difficult choices. It is all too true that crime and violence are deeply rooted. The philosophy of "I'm going to get mine now anyway I can" is a strong incentive for instant gratification by any means necessary. [35]

[1] boils down to： 日本語の「詰まるところ」と同じイメージ.
when all is said and done： 結局のところ

[5] Black Panther Party： 1966年にオークランドで，ボビー・シール，ヒューイ・ニュートンを中心に結成された，革命のための反=非暴力組織．黒の皮ジャン，黒パンツ，黒のベレー帽のいでたちで，各自銃をたずさえ，ユニットを組んで行動した．一方ではコミュニティの「生存プログラム」を実践．子供たちに無料の昼食を与えたり，医療検診に力を注いだ．

[6] 10-point program and platform： "What We Want, What We Believe" と題された黒豹党の綱領には以下の10項目の要求が並んでいた．① 自由(自分たちの運命を決する権力)，② 黒人人民の完全雇用，③ 資本家によるコミュニティ搾取の終わり，④ 人間にふさわしい住居，⑤ 腐敗したアメリカ社会の本質を明らかにする教育，⑥ 兵役免除，⑦ 警察による黒人住民への残虐行為 (police brutality) の終わり，⑧ 監獄からの黒人同胞の解放，⑨ 黒人が黒人陪審員によって裁かれること，⑩ 世界の黒人の民族自決が国連で保証されること．

[9] awaken our people： 11行目には "wake folks up" とある．かつて「闘争」は，惑わされている大衆を目覚めさせることに力点が置かれたものです．

[15] manufactured negroes who were placed in front of us in order to pacify the community： 黒人社会を平穏に治めるために白人が遣わした，彼らのいいなりになるように仕立て上げられた黒人．1965年夏のロサンジェルス・ワッツ地区の暴動に際して，非暴力を訴えに出かけたキング牧師などが，この範疇に入る．

[21] confronted it in a direct manly fashion： 現代の黒人フェミニストから攻撃されそうな「父権的」精神が，このエッセイ全体に感じとれるのはたしかだ．

[22] would have wanted： 黒豹党の精神的支柱であり続けたマルコムが暗殺されたのは1965年．党の活動が始まる前年のことだった．

[24] The established order depends on disorganization, demoralization, disunity and defeatism： 我々が組織としてのまとまりに欠け，意気が低く，バラバラで，敗北主義に染まっていることの上に，既成権力が機能しているのだ

[27] unit： 黒豹党はメンバーを軍隊式にユニットに分けて組織活動を展開した．

[30] viable： (単に理念上のものではなく)現実に有効な

[35] by any means necessary：「必要ないかなる手段を講じても」というのは，マルコムが訴えた黒人解放の戦闘的キャッチフレーズ．その大切な言葉を「刹那的満足感」を得ようとする輩がだらしなく使っているという嘆きが，ここにはこもっている．

It is used as an excuse for all kinds of negative actions. But the
future doesn't lie in that direction. I become very depressed when
I see kids cutting school and laughing about it. They think they
are getting away with something when the truth is they're falling
into a predictable trap by dropping out before they're even get- [5]
ting started.

You see most of these kids don't have the proper guidance at
home to prevent this madness. They're going to live in the same
world as my son and his friends. Common sense demands that
they be saved from self-immolation. If they burn then everyone is [10]
going to burn. They'll take down a lot of others with them. Those
of us who know better must do better. That is why my friends and
I have reorganized the old Black Panther newspaper. We know
that we must get the word out to our many communities.

The word is very simple. It's up to us to save ourselves. No one [15]
else is going to do it for us. Our community response to nihilism
is positive action, job creation and the reestablishment of the family as the basic building block of society. We have allowed ourselves to stagnate in this regard. I get very angry when I see
people abdicate their responsibility as humans and parents. They [20]
want to pretend that someone else is responsible for their lives.
That they are not in charge of their own actions. Well that's just
not the case. We are all responsible for what we do. Always have
been. I don't know if my frustration is coming across. You see I
know we can do better. It's not normal for teenage girls to be [25]
mothers before they leave high school. There's too much of this
going on because people don't think about the consequences of
their actions. It can only be stopped if we emphasize the downside of teenage pregnancies. This can be done best within the con-
fines of the family structure. [30]

This is what I've tried to do in my own family. This is my second marriage. My wife is from the West Indies and I have a 14
year old stepson. My two boys will always hear about personal
responsibility from me. It goes with the turf of being a man. When
they start their own families they should understand that it's up [35]

[3] cutting school and laughing about it: 学校をさぼっても(悔いるどころか)ヘラヘラしている

[4] getting away with something: うまいことやって何かを逃れる. *You can't say that to her and get away with it.* (そんなこと彼女に言ったらただじゃすまないぞ)

[5] get(ting) started: 世の中に出ていく

[7] You see most of these . . . : 以下しだいに文章が熱っぽく，思いのままを会話体で綴るスタイルになっていく．この文も，You seeの次にカンマがない方が，彼のたたみかけるようなしゃべり方の特徴がよく出る気がする．

[9] Common sense demands . . . : 誰だってそう願わずにはいられない

[10] self-immolation: みすみす自分の人生を投げ捨てること
burn: 「焼けこげる」とは，具体的にはドラッグに溺れたり，15歳で妊娠したり，銃で殺し合ったりすること．

[12] know better: are more sensible
do better: take sensible actions

[13] reorganized the old Black Panther newspaper: かつて党が活動していた時代の機関誌は，1991年春，"Black Panther: Black Community News Service"として再刊された．

[17] positive action: 積極的差別是正措置
job creation: コミュニティの経済的活性化による就労の促進

[18] the basic building block of society: 社会の基本構成要素
allowed ourselves to stagnate: がんばりが足らずに停滞に陥ってしまった

[22] That they are not in charge of their own actions: 自分がこういうことをするのは自分じゃない誰かの責任なのだと

[24] if my frustration is coming across: 私の苛立ちが伝わってくれているかどうか
I know: knowに強勢．「自信をもって言える」．

[26] There's too much of this going on: まわり中こんなことばっかりだ

[28] downside: マイナス面

[34] It goes with the turf of being a man: 男としてどう生きていくかという問題とつながっている．

[35] it's up to them to set the pace: みずから家族の模範となるように生きていくのが自分らの責任だ．up to: the duty or responsibility of

to them to set the pace. They're responsible for the tone of their families and by extension the tone of their communities. They will be judged by the job that they do or don't do. You see if we can take credit for our successes (the civil rights movement, the liberation of Africa, etc.) then we must be willing to shoulder blame for our failures (broken families, crime, poor schools, and so on). These are some of the issues that worry me as I march through middle age.

Isn't that something, man? When you first met me I was in my early 30's and not worried about too much of anything, least of all the next generation. I figured that things would work out one way or another. Well, I guess they do but it helps a whole lot if you have a personal reason for seeing that they do. In my case the personal reason is my family.

[1] responsible for the tone of their families : ちなみに，この間オークランドの彼の新しいアパートをブランデーを下げて訪れたら，ポールは酒もタバコもやめていた．

[2] by extension : 広げて言えば

[4] take credit for : ～を自分たちの手柄にする

the liberation of Africa : （1960年代に大きく進展した）アフリカ諸国の独立達成

[5] shoulder blame : 批判を背負う

[9] Isn't that something, man? : なにか感慨深いことを言ったりするときによく口をつく文句．something は「なかなかたいしたこと」の意．man は黒人たちが使う，親しみのこもった呼びかけで，もともとは白人から boy と呼ばれることに対する反発がこもっていた．60年代以降，白人の若者たちにもヒップな言い方として浸透している．

[11] work out one way or another : とにかくどうにかなる

[12] helps a whole lot : 事がずっとうまく進む

[13] seeing that they do : 物事が work out するように手を尽くす

SESSION 5

Books of My Life

■

Steve Erickson

AS A CHILD I was enthralled by the Oz books of L. Frank Baum, particularly *Ozma of Oz* and *Rinki-Tink of Oz*. These were more than just fairy tales, they were turn-of-the-century, prenuclear updates of all the roiling, primal fears and wonders that inform fairy tales, and Baum was the first home-grown [5] American surrealist. I particularly remember the scene in which Dorothy sneaks into the chamber of the beautiful queen only to find a huge glass cabinet filled with a hundred heads, all of them belonging to the queen and worn according on her whim. As an adolescent I obsessively read comic books, much to my mother's [10] dismay, until suddenly at the age of fifteen I cast them aside as a childish thing, and also because the adventures inside so rarely lived up to what the covers seemed to promise, or the adventures I created in my own head from that first image.

In my late adolescence and early twenties, when a novelist's [15] sensibility comes of age, I first became aware of the three writers who had the greatest impact on my life and work. The first was William Faulkner, who taught me about structure, the way it was more just than the mechanical frame of a story but rather the emotional landscape, the way a world is created not according to the [20] clock of time but the clock of memory, such as in *The Sound and the Fury* or "The Bear" in *Go Down Moses*. Distinctions between inte-

リチャード・パワーズ，ウィリアム・ヴォルマンらと並んで，そのスケールの大きさ，想像力の強靭さにおいて，80～90 年代アメリカ文学の最重要作家である（と僕は思う）スティーヴ・エリクソン．どういう読書体験が，『黒い時計の旅』（福武文庫）をはじめとする，ウィリアム・フォークナーがラテンアメリカ文学とサイエンス・フィクションを経由したような大作を生んだのか．その問いに答えてくれるのがこの文章である．1992 年，文芸書評誌『リテレール』（メタローグ社）の当時の編集長，安原顯の依頼を受けて書かれた．🅛

[1] Oz books of L. Frank Baum： 1900 年刊行の *The Wonderful Wizard of Oz*（『オズの魔法使い』）にはじまり，ボームはオズ・シリーズを 14 冊書いた．

[3] turn-of-the-century： 文字どおりには「世紀の変わり目の」だが，実際には特に，19 世紀末から 20 世紀初頭について使われることが多い．

[4] prenuclear： 「核以前の」．エリクソンにとって，核以前か以後かでは，「アメリカ」の意味も大きく変わってくる．彼にとって核とは基本的に，アメリカの「無垢の終わり」を意味する．
updates： 新バージョン
roiling： 混沌とした

[5] inform： 「知らせる」ではなく，「～に充満している」
the first home-grown American surrealist： シュルレアリスムといえば，ヨーロッパ中心のムーブメントとして普通考えられ，アメリカはあまり顧みられない．

[9] according on her whim： 女王の気の向くままに

[10] obsessively： 憑かれたように

[13] live(d) up to： ～に十分応える

[16] come(s) of age： 成人する，成熟をみる

[18] William Faulkner： 20 世紀世界文学最大の作家の 1 人（1897–1962）．
the way it was more just than . . .： この部分も，20 行の the way a world is . . . の部分も，who taught me からつなげて読む．

[20] not according to the clock of time but the clock of memory： 思いきって単純化すれば，フォークナーにせよエリクソンにせよ，時計の時間が 10 年経とうが 100 年経とうが，意味ある出来事が起きなければ，そのあいだの時間はなかったにも等しい．そしてまた，50 年経とうが 100 年経とうが，決定的な出来事は，記憶のなかで現在として生きつづける．

[21] *The Sound and the Fury* or “The Bear” . . .： いずれもフォークナーの作品．特に *The Sound and the Fury* (1929) 第 1 章の，白痴ベンジーの内的独白から成る章は，直線的時間を徹底的に解体する試みとして有名．

rior and exterior life in Faulkner's novels were exposed as capricious and trivial; questions of which was more "real" were revealed to be meaningless and even deluded. Faulkner's great characters were both metaphors and real lives, transcendent in the first case and detailed with psychological specificity in the [5] second — Joe Christmas, that cipher of rage and passion in *Light in August* who literally does not know if he is a black man or white, and therefore embodies everything that's hopeful and damned about America.

The second writer to have great impact on me was Henry [10] Miller. I was electrified by *Tropic of Cancer*, not its sexuality, which by the early 1970s didn't seem particularly scandalous, but rather its emotional nakedness, the way the book razed, from its opening passages, the artifice and conceit of literature: "I have no money, no resources, no hopes. I am the happiest man alive. A [15] year ago, six months ago, I thought that I was an artist. I no longer think about it, I *am* . . . . This is not a book. This is libel, slander, defamation of character . . . this is a prolonged insult, a gob of spit in the face of Art, a kick in the pants to God, Man, Destiny, Time, Love, Beauty . . . ." Miller's insistence on integrating the lyrical [20] with the vulgar, the cosmos with the gutter, meant that all the youthful ideas I had about what art was — about its preciousness, about its rarefaction — had to be abandoned if I was to go on as a writer. And so I abandoned them and, retaining the few things about my early writing that were truly and essentially me, [25] went on.

The third writer was Bob Dylan. Dylan is easily the single most important writer of my generation. His records *Highway 61 Revisited, Blonde on Blonde* and *The Basement Tapes* are great American novels, surreal journeys through American frontier towns and [30] women's bedchambers, and when I say they are great novels I don't mean just the words of these records. I mean the sound of them. It is the whole sound of the records in which lies Dylan's narrative power — the organ and guitars and drums, the words and, perhaps above all, Dylan's voice. Once again, as with [35]

[1] capricious: 単なる空想の

[2] questions of which was more "real": この部分がこのセンテンスの主語.

[3] deluded: 迷妄にすぎない

[4] both metaphors and real lives: metaphorsであるということは, 自分自身とは違う, 何か普遍的なものを体現しているということであり, real livesであるということは, 生身の人間としてもリアリティを持っているということ.
transcendent in the first case: in the first casesは言い換えれば "as metaphors" ということ (このあとのin the secondは "as real lives"). transcendentは普通「超越的」と訳され, 日常的な束縛を超えたものを言い表わすのに使う.

[6] that cipher of rage and passion in *Light in August*: *Light in August*はフォークナー代表作のひとつ(1932). 自分に黒人の血が混じっているかもしれないという謎を抱え込んだ人物ジョー・クリスマスの荒々しい感情のうねり(rage and passion)が, アメリカという国家が抱え込んだ矛盾と希望を読みとくための暗号(cipher)になっている.

[9] damned: 呪われた

[11] I was electrified by *Tropic of Cancer*, not its sexuality . . . : ヘンリー・ミラー(1891–1980)の処女作 *Tropic of Cancer* (1934)は当初パリで刊行され, アメリカでは即発禁になり, 60年代に入って最高裁が「猥褻ならず」という判決を下すまで刊行されなかった. いまでもミラーというと,「性を赤裸々に描いた作家」というイメージがつきまとう.

[13] razed: completely destroyed

[14] artifice and conceit: (わざとらしい)技巧や, 思い上がり

[17] libel, slander, defamation of character: 罵倒, 中傷, 人格毀損

[18] prolonged: えんえんと続く a gob of spit: 唾のかたまり

[19] a kick in the pants: 尻への一蹴り

[20] integrating the lyrical with the vulgar: 叙情的なものと野卑なものを(すなわち, 普通なら正反対と考えられるものを)統合すること. 次のthe cosmos and the gutter (宇宙とドブ)も同じ.

[22] preciousness . . . rarefaction: 尊さ, 高尚さ

[25] were truly and essentially me: 本当に根っから私である

[27] Bob Dylan: アメリカン・ロック最大のシンガー・ソングライター(1941–).
easily: without doubt

[28] *Highway 61 Revisited* . . . : 3つとも60年代に録音されたディラン代表作.

[33] in which lies Dylan's narrative power: この部分の主語は "Dylan's narrative power" (語り手としてのディランの力). なおエリクソンがこのほかに「影響源」として挙げているロック・ミュージシャンは, ヴァン・モリソン, レイ・チャー

Faulkner and Miller, Dylan changed how I thought about art, how I thought about myself as a writer. These artists were important not for what they reinforced but the upheaval they caused in my life, and how nothing was possible after I read them except to cast away pre-conceived notions, or things that were just as child- [5] ish as the comic books I gave up at the age of fifteen.

The Significant Others of my reading life were those who reinforced the old lessons, or brought my literary identity into focus. Gabriel García Márquez, who taught me that the lessons of Faulkner could be applied to my own experience as naturally as [10] Márquez applied them to his. Philip K. Dick, who raised in his best books first the question of the nature of reality and later, more importantly, the question of the nature of humanity followed by, almost incidentally, the nature of God. Stendhal, who interwove the concerns of politics with the conflicts of the psyche, [15] and Emily Brontë, whose *Wuthering Heights* is one of the most subversive Western novels ever written, upending the nineteenth century's frantic effort to contain people's passions. The sweeping, delirious last third of Melville's *Moby Dick,* and the great American crime writers James M. Cain and Raymond Chandler [20] and Jim Thompson. The poetry of Rimbaud and Baudelaire and Pablo Neruda, and an early Japanese novel called *Kokoro,* which astonished me for its emotional precision (and in translation yet!) and the way it preceded the existential tenor of the French thirty years later (in comparison to which the French seem almost glib, [25] shallow). And after having learned these lessons, I can now return to my childhood every once in a while and, almost thirty years later, read a comic book, by artists I assume have learned similar things: Alan Moore and Neil Gaiman, Frank Miller and Art Spiegelman and the Hernandez Brothers. [30]

ルズ，ジョン・レノン，ルー・リード，ドアーズ，オーティス・レディング，ブルース・スプリングスティーン，ニール・ヤング，ビートルズなど．

[3] reinforce(d)： (すでにあるものを)強化する
upheaval： great change, with much confusion and violence
[4] how nothing was possible . . .： how 以下はその前の the upheaval they caused in my life と同格．how はわかりにくければ the fact と読み替えてもだいたい同じ．nothing was possible . . . except to 〜 は「〜するほかなかった」
[5] pre-conceived： 出来合いの
[7] The Significant Others： 行動や考え方に大きな影響を及ぼす(及ぼした)他人．
[9] Gabriel García Márquez： コロンビアの作家 (1928–)．60〜70年代に隆盛だったラテンアメリカ文学の代表的存在．
[11] Márquez applied them to his： ガルシア＝マルケスがフォークナーに影響されたことは周知の事実．
Philip K. Dick： 現実と虚構の錯綜をテーマとした傑作 SF 多数 (1928–82)．
[14] almost incidentally： ほとんどついでといった感じで
[15] interwove： 織り合わせる
the psyche： [sáiki]「頭」よりも「魂」に近い意味での「精神」
[17] subversive： 破壊的な　upend(ing)： ひっくり返す
[18] frantic effort： 懸命の努力　contain： 閉じこめる，鎮める
The sweeping, delirious last third of Melville's *Moby Dick*： "sweeping, delirious" は「すべてを巻き込んで進む，言葉が激しく噴き出る」といった感じ．メルヴィル (1819–91) の大作『白鯨』(1851) の最後の 3 分の 1 は，復讐の念に燃えるエイハブ船長とモビー・ディックとの対決をめぐる長大な描写が中心．
[20] James M. Cain . . .： いずれも代表的なアメリカのミステリー作家．エリクソンの都市の描き方には，どこかミステリー的なタッチが感じられる．
[21] Rimbaud and Baudelaire and Pablo Neruda： ランボー (1854–91) とボードレール (1821–67) はフランス，ネルーダ (1904–73) はチリの，いずれも著名な詩人．
[23] in translation yet!： しかも翻訳で！
[24] precede(d)： 〜に先行する
the existential tenor： 実存主義的傾向．サルトル，カミュらの，不条理な世界のなかでの人間の自由の問題を追求した文学を念頭に置いて言っている．
[25] glib, shallow： どちらも「薄っぺらで中味がない」
[29] Alan Moore and Neil Gaiman . . .： 現代アメリカの漫画家たち．日本でもよく知られているのは，父親が生き抜いたアウシュビッツの体験を漫画にした『マウス』(晶文社) のアート・スピーゲルマン．

スティーヴ・エリクソン(写真・久家靖秀)

Steve Erickson, *Books of My Life*

The Arabian Nights
15 世紀アラビアで完成した，永遠の物語の宝庫.

Psychotic Reactions and Carburetor Dung, Lester Bangs
夭折した異色の評論家によるロック評論集.

Les Fleurs du Mal, Baudelaire
『悪の華』(1857，筑摩書房『ボードレール全集』など). エリクソンの *Arc d'X* (『X のアーチ』) には，これをもじった Fleurs d'X (X の華) というストリップ酒場が出てくる.

Ozma of Oz, L. Frank Baum
『オズのオズマ姫』(ハヤカワ文庫).

The Eye of the Beholder, Marc Behm
アメリカのミステリー作家によるスリラー(1980).

The Dream Songs, John Berryman
実験的作風を持った戦後アメリカ最大級の詩人による，韻文小説とも称される超長篇詩(合本最終版 1969).

Unseen America: The Greatest Cult Exploitation Magazines 1950–1966, Alan Betrock
50–60 年代ティーンエイジ文化の専門家による，トラッシュ雑誌(三文雑誌)決定版ソースブック.

The Complete Poems of William Blake
ブレイクは 18 世紀最大の英国幻視詩人. 1960 年代アメリカ幻覚文化にも大きな影響を与えている.

Labyrinths, Jorge Luis Borges
60 年代アメリカで出た，アルゼンチンの偉大な短篇作家ボルヘス(1899–1986)の選集.

The Sheltering Sky, Paul Bowles

長年タンジールに住む異色アメリカ人小説家ボウルズ (1910–) の長篇 (1949). 『シェルタリング・スカイ』(新潮文庫).

The Secret Paris of the '30s, Brassaï

モンパルナスの夜の妖しい魅力を捉えたブラッサイの写真集 (1933). 『未知のパリ, 深夜のパリ』(みすず書房).

Thomas Jefferson : An Intimate History, Fawn Brodie

トマス・ジェファソンが奴隷のサリー・ヘミングズと実は愛人関係にあったと主張するスキャンダラスな歴史書. エリクソンが『X のアーチ』を書く上でインスピレーション源になった書物のひとつ.

Wuthering Heights, Emily Brontë

『嵐が丘』(1847). ヨークシャーの荒涼たる地を背景に, 悪魔的なまでに烈しい男女の愛とその悲劇を描く.

The Parade's Gone By, Kevin Brownlow

映画研究家ブラウンロウが 1983 年に出した, 映画史への讃歌.

Serenade, James M. Cain

『郵便配達は二度ベルを鳴らす』で知られるジェームズ・M・ケインの第二作 (1937). おちぶれた白人アメリカ人歌手と, メキシコ人女性との叶わぬ愛を扱う.

Journey to the End of the Night, Céline

フランスの作家セリーヌ (1894–1961) による, 文学の概念を根本から覆す破格の小説 (1932). 『夜の果ての旅』(中公文庫).

The Selected Writings of Blaise Cendrars

サンドラールはスイスのフランス語詩人, 作家 (1887–1961).

The Long Goodbye, Raymond Chandler

ミステリー作家チャンドラーの代表作 (1954). チャンドラーの描くロサンゼルスは, エリクソンのロサンゼルスにも影を落としていると思われる. 『長いお別れ』(ハヤカワ文庫).

The Names, Don DeLillo

現代アメリカの重厚派作家として高い評価を保つデリーロ (1936–) が, ギリシャ中東のカルト教団をテーマにして書いた小説 (1982).

A Scanner Darkly, Philip K. Dick

ドラッグに溺れた友人たちへのオマージュ(1977).『暗闇のスキャナー』(創元 SF 文庫)

The Transmigration of Timothy Archer, Philip K. Dick

『ティモシー・アーチャーの転生』(創元 SF 文庫). 救済を求める人間たちのドラマ.

Crime and Punishment, Fyodor Dostoyevsky

『罪と罰』(1866).

The Alexandria Quartet, Lawrence Durrell

イギリスの作家ロレンス・ダレル(1912–)による四部作(1957–60).『ジュスティーヌ』『バルタザール』『マウントオリーヴ』『クレア』(河出書房新社).

Invisible Man, Ralph Ellison

アメリカの作家ラルフ・エリソン(1914–94)の唯一の小説(1952). 白人中心の社会にあって「見えない」存在として扱われる黒人のありようを問う.『見えない人間』(早川書房).

The Black Dahlia, James Ellroy

エリクソンとも交友のあるミステリー作家による, 殺された美女のイメージに憑かれて破滅していく男たちの物語.『ブラック・ダリア』(文藝春秋).

A Fan's Notes, Frederick Exley

1968年, エリクソンが18歳の年にフォークナー賞を受賞した, 暗いトーンの魂の放浪記.

Go Down, Moses, William Faulkner

白人文明到来以前の南部の森を神秘的に描き出す中篇「熊」を含む, たがいに連結した物語集(1942).『行け, モーセ』(富山房).

Light in August, William Faulkner

本文参照.『八月の光』(新潮文庫).

The Sound and the Fury, William Faulkner

本文参照.『響きと怒り』(富山房).

Tender is the Night, F. Scott Fitzgerald

20世紀前半のアメリカの代表的作家による, 喪失と破滅の美しく哀しい物語(1934).『夜はやさし』(角川文庫).

Red Harvest, Dashiell Hammett

ハードボイルドというジャンルを「発明」した画期的長篇(1929).『赤い収穫』(ハヤカワ文庫, 創元推理文庫).

Human Disastrophism, Gilbert Hernandez

本文にも言及のあったヘルナンデス三兄弟のうちの一人によるコミックス.

Berlin Stories, Christopher Isherwood

イギリスの作家イシャウッド(1904–86)による，ヒトラー台頭前夜のベルリンの雰囲気をあざやかに捉えた連作(1935–39)．エリクソンの『黒い時計の旅』にもその影響は色濃い．3冊のうち1冊のみ既訳(『救いなき人々』文藝春秋)．

The Sacred Night, Tahar Ben Jelloun

最近日本でも翻訳が出て話題を呼んでいる，モロッコ人作家ターハル・ベン＝ジェルーン(1944–　)による世界的ベストセラー．『聖なる夜』(紀伊國屋書店)．

Dubliners, James Joyce

アイルランドの大作家初期の連作短篇(1914)．『ダブリン市民』(新潮文庫)．のちの『フィネガンズ・ウェイク』などとは違い，基本的にはリアリズム色が濃い．

Reeling, Pauline Kael

辛口の映画批評家による評論集．

The Selected Stories of Franz Kafka

英語圏でももっとも有名なカフカ短篇はやはり「変身」．

Fear and Trembling, Sören Kierkegaard

デンマークの哲学者キルケゴール(1813–55)の著作(1843)．『おそれとおののき』(白水社)．

The Book of Lilith, Barbara Black Koltuv

ユング派心理学者による，古代神話の女悪霊リリスの研究書．この強力な霊の力を各自が心のなかに統合する必要を訴える．

The Unbearable Lightness of Being, Milan Kundera

チェコの国際派作家クンデラ(1929–　)の代表作(1984)．『存在の耐えられない軽さ』(集英社)．

Magnetic Fields, Ron Loewinsohn

ビート作家らと交流をもち，バークレーでも教えていたイメージの職人による秀作．

The Selected Poems of Federico García Lorca

ロルカは今世紀スペインの代表的詩人(1898–1936)．

The Heart Is a Lonely Hunter, Carson McCullers

一人の聾唖者が，孤独な人々をはからずも引き寄せてしまう物語．アメリカ南部の女性作家マッカラーズのデビュー作(1940)．『心は孤独な狩人』(新潮文庫，絶版)

Mystery Train, Greil Marcus

ロック評論を文化研究のレベルに高めた記念碑的作品．『ミステリー・トレイン』(第三文明社)．

One Hundred Years of Solitude, Gabriel García Márquez

現実と幻想の錯綜する壮大な語りによって，一族の栄枯盛衰の歴史を描く．『百年の孤独』(新潮社)．

Moby Dick, Herman Melville

本文参照.『白鯨』(新潮文庫, 岩波文庫等).

The Cosmological Eye, Henry Miller

はじめてアメリカで出たヘンリー・ミラーの作品 (1939).『宇宙の眼』(新潮文庫).

Tropic of Cancer, Henry Miller

本文参照.『北回帰線』(新潮文庫).

Watchmen, Alan Moore and Dave Gibbons

反ユートピア的世界を舞台に, 既成のスーパーヒーロー像を転倒させたようなキャラクターたちが登場するコミックス (1986–87).

My Secret Life, Anonymous

ポルノグラフィーの古典.『わが秘密の生涯』(富士見ロマン文庫).

Five Decades: Poems 1925–1970, Pablo Neruda

本文にも出てきたネルーダ (1904–73) の詩大全.

The Complete Stories of Flannery O'Connor

アメリカの奇妙なカトリック作家オコナー (1925–64) の短篇集.『フラナリー・オコナー短編集』(新潮文庫).

Appointment in Samara, John O'Hara

アメリカの作家オハラ (1905–70) の出世作 (1934). 裕福な人々の世界を諷刺的に描く.『サマーラの町で会おう』(集英社).

The Collected Essays of George Orwell

オーウェルは『1984年』などで有名なイギリスの作家・評論家 (1903–50).

Remembrance of Things Past, Marcel Proust

20世紀文学最大の成果のひとつといわれる, フランスの作家プルースト (1871–1922) によるきわめて長大な自伝的小説 (1913–27).『失われた時を求めて』(新潮社, ちくま文庫).

V., Thomas Pynchon

現代アメリカ最大の作家ピンチョン (1937–) のデビュー作 (1963). 謎の女Vをめぐって展開する錯綜した物語, とひとまず強引にまとめてしまっていいかな?『V.』(国書刊行会).

Illuminations, Arthur Rimbaud

ランボー (1854–91) が10代終わりから20代はじめにかけて書いた詩を集めた本 (1886).『イリュミナシオン』(筑摩書房).

The Rise and Fall of the Third Reich, William L. Shirer

ナチスの興亡をたどる古典的歴史書 (1960). エリクソンの『黒い時計の旅』の冒頭にも引用されている.『第三帝国の興亡』(東京創元社, 絶版).

Kokoro, Natsume Soseki

エリクソンは思春期のある晩に『嵐が丘』を読み, 次の晩に『こころ』を読んだという．あんな強烈な読書体験はなかったと本人も言っていた．

The Red and the Black, Stendhal

『赤と黒』(新潮文庫等)．

More Than Human, Theodore Sturgeon

社会から追放された6人が，孤独と困難のなかでたがいの心を合体させ超人化する，SF作家スタージョンの最高傑作(1953)．『人間以上』(ハヤカワ文庫)．

The Collected Poems of Dylan Thomas

激しく生きながら幻視的な詩を書きつづけたウェールズ出身の詩人の「選集」出版は1952年．その精神は，彼の名を冠したアメリカのフォーク歌手に受け継がれた．主な詩は『ディラン・トマス詩集』(小沢書店) に訳されている．

Savage Night, Jim Thompson

トンプソンは1950年代から60年代にかけて犯罪小説を多く書き，80年代に入って再評価された．

Cane, Jean Toomer

アメリカの黒人作家トゥーマー(1894–1967)による，詩，小説，戯曲を織りまぜてアメリカの黒人の体験を伝えた作品．

The Ogre, Michel Tournier

フランスの作家トゥルニエ(1924–　)の小説(1970)．魔王や食人鬼の棲む神話的世界を現代に移植したような物語．『魔王』(二見書房)．

The Death Ship, B. Traven

生涯正体を隠しつづけた作家B・トレイヴン(1969没)の小説(1925)．

The Adventures of Huckleberry Finn, Mark Twain

マーク・トウェインによる19世紀アメリカ小説の古典(1884)．『ハックルベリー・フィンの冒険』(岩波文庫等)．

The Letters to Theo, Vincent Van Gogh

ゴッホ(1853–90)の芸術を知る上で貴重な資料とされる，弟への書簡集．『ファン・ゴッホ書簡全集』(みすず書房)．

Shadow Dancing in the USA, Michael Ventura

エリクソンの友人による奔放なエッセイ．

The Burnt Orange Heresy, Charles Willeford

描写シーンの鮮烈さで人気の高い作家の異色犯罪小説．

The Selected Poems of William Carlos Williams

ウィリアムズはアメリカ20世紀前半の代表的詩人．

The Collected Poems of William Butler Yeats

イェイツはアイルランド20世紀前半の代表的詩人．

SESSION 6

Farwell

■

Stuart Dybek

TONIGHT, A STEADY drizzle, streetlights smoldering in fog like funnels of light collecting rain. Down Farwell, the balcony windows of the apartment building where my friend Babovitch once lived, reflected across the wet tennis courts, and I wondered if I would ever leave this city. I remembered the first [5] night I walked down Farwell to visit Babo. He was teaching a class in Russian literature that I was taking, and had invited me over. I'd never had a teacher invite me to his home before. "When's a good time?" I asked.

"I can *always* use the company," he answered, scrawling out his [10] address. "There's no phone."

It was a winter night, snowing. His apartment building was the last one on the block where the street dead-ended against the lake. Behind a snow-clotted cyclone fence, the tennis courts were drifted over, and beyond the courts and a small, lakeside park, a [15] white pier extended to a green beacon. Snow had obliterated the outlines of sidewalks and curbs and that night the pier looked as if it was a continuation of the street, as if Farwell lengthened out into the lake. I walked out toward the beacon. Ice, sculpted by waves and spray, encrusted the pier. The guard cables and bea- [20] con tower were sheathed in ice. In the frozen quiet, I could hear the lake rasping in under the floes and feel the pier shudder, and

シカゴの，どちらかというと侘しい下町をめぐる小説を書きつづける作家スチュアート・ダイベック．でもその情景には不思議といつも，神の恩寵のような「なつかしさ」(彼の好きな日本語) が漂っている．これを読んで気に入って下さった方は，ぜひ *The Coast of Chicago* (Picador USA)，または邦訳(拙訳で恐縮ですが)『シカゴ育ち』(白水社 U ブックス)をどうぞ．Ⓛ

[1] drizzle： 霧雨　smolder(ing)： 普通は何かが燃えて「くすぶる」ことをいう．

[2] funnels of light： 光のじょうご．

[4] reflected across . . .： reflected の意味上の主語は the balcony windows. テニスコートが濡れて鏡のようになって，そこに窓が映っている．

[10] I can *always* use the company： 「お客はいつだって歓迎さ」．can (あるいは could) use ～ は「～があるとありがたい」．*I could use a drink!* (一杯やりたいね!)
scrawl(ing) out： 殴り書きする

[13] block： 角から角までが 1 ブロック．アメリカで町なかの距離を言うときの普通の単位．*My office is only two blocks from here — why don't you come over?*
the street dead-ended against the lake： Farwell という通りはシカゴに実在し，事実湖につきあたって行き止まりになる．

[14] a snow-clotted cyclone fence： 雪がこびりついた金網．cyclone fence は運動場などでよく見る，菱形の並んだ普通の金網．
were drifted over： 雪が吹き寄せていた

[15] a white pier extended to a green beacon： pier は「桟橋」，beacon は「灯台」

[16] obliterated： covered completely

[17] curbs：「縁石」と訳され，歩道と車道の仕切りに(日本ならガードレールがあったりするところに)敷かれた石．

[18] lengthened out into the lake： そのまま湖のなかまで延びていた

[19] sculpted by waves and spray： 波やしぶきに削られて．sculpture といえば彫刻のことで，ここでも氷に彫刻のイメージが付与されている．

[20] encrust(ed)： 何か固いもので覆うことを言う．crust といえばパイ皮．
guard cables： 安全用の金属ケーブル

[21] sheath(ed)： 前行の encrusted とほぼ同じ (sheath は刀のさや)．sculpted，あるいはこのあとの frozen といった言葉とともに，何もかもが硬い氷に包まれた感じが強調されている．

[22] rasp(ing)： きしる．rasp は本来「やすり」の意味で，ここでもやすりをかける音をイメージしていい．
floes： 浮氷　shudder： ぶるっと震える

as I walked back toward the apartment building I thought I heard singing.

The baritone voice resonating across the tennis courts seemed to float from a balcony window where a curtain fluttered out as if signalling. I was sure it was Babo's window. Instead of ringing [5] his bell, I stood on the tennis court and tried to make out the song, but the words were indistinct. I formed a snowball out of fresh snow — snow too feathery to be good packing — and lobbed it at the window. It exploded against the pane with a soft *phoom.* I expected Babo to come to the window. Instead, the music stopped. I [10] lobbed another snowball and the bronze light inside the apartment flicked off. Finally, I walked around to the entrance hall and buzzed the bell beside the name Andrei Babovitch, but there was no answer. I was about to give up when I saw his face magnified by the beveled panes of the lobby door. He opened the door and [15] broke into the craggy grin I'd seen possess his face in class when he would read a poem aloud — first in Russian, as if chanting, and then translated into his hesitant, British-accented English.

"So, you," he said.

"Is it a good night for a visit?" [20]

"Definitely. Come in, please. Have tea. And a little shot of something to warm up."

"I thought I guessed which window was yours and threw snowballs to get your attention."

"That was *you*! I thought hooligans had heard Chaliapin moan- [25] ing about fate and become enraged. Russian opera can have that effect even on those not addicted to rock and roll. I didn't know what to expect next — a brick, maybe — so I turned off the music and laid down on the floor in the dark."

"Sorry," I said, "I wasn't thinking — I don't know why I didn't [30] just ring the bell."

"No, no. It would have been a memorable entrance. I'm sorry I missed it, though if I looked out the window and saw you in the dark I still might have thought it was hooligans," he laughed. "As you see, my nerves aren't what they should be." [35]

[3] resonating : 反響している

[4] flutter(ed) out : 外に向かってはためく

[6] tried to make out the song : どんな歌か聞き取ろうとした．make out はわかりにくい音を聞き取ったり，わかりにくい字を読み取ったりする行為についていう．*I just can't make out this handwriting.*（この筆跡，さっぱり読めない）

[7] indistinct : not clear

[8] too feathery to be good packing : 雪合戦を真剣にやったことのある方ならおわかりだろうが，降ったばかり (fresh) の雪は，よく締まった雪玉 (good packing) を作るにはふわふわ (feathery) すぎる．

lob(bed) : テニスなどで「ロビング」という形で日本語にも定着している．ゆるい球を高く打ち(投げ)上げること．

[9] pane : 窓ガラス soft *phoom* : 雪が窓にあった音を文字にしている．

[12] flicked off : パッと消えた

[13] buzz(ed) : er をつければ buzzer（ブザーのこと）．ただし発音は [bʌz].

the bell beside the name Andrei Bavobitch : アメリカのアパートではたいてい，玄関に各世帯のブザーが並んでいる．

[15] beveled panes : 四辺に斜角をつけたガラス．ドアにはめ込んだ厚めのガラス．

[16] craggy grin : いかつい，にやっという笑い顔．craggy は，山などで「岩の多い」という意味が一番一般的．

I'd seen possess his face in class . . . : この部分はすべて craggy grin にかかる．このいかつい笑いが，教室で，彼の顔にとり憑く (possess) のを「僕」は見たことがあった (I'd seen) ということ．

[17] as if chanting : 呪文でも唱えるように

[19] "So, you" : 「やあ，君だったか」ということだが，ここに限らず，バボヴィッチの喋り方はいつも何となく外国人的．

[21] shot : 「ショットバー」といった言い方で日本語にもなっている．a shot of vodka など，強い酒の方が似合う表現（a shot of beer とは言わない）．

[25] hooligans : 近年はイギリスの暴力的なサッカーファンの意味が定着してしまったが，本来はごろつき，無頼漢一般を指す語．

Chaliapin : 一世を風靡したロシアのバス歌手．『ボリス・ゴドゥノフ』をはじめロシアオペラにおいて特に高い評価を得た．雪の降る夜，おそらくはすり切れたレコードから出てくるその朗々たる声が運命を嘆く (moaning about fate) のが開け放たれた窓から聞こえてくる，という情景を考えただけで楽しい．

[26] become enraged : 激怒したのはシャリアピンではなく，hooligans. 前行の had からつながる．

[32] It would have been a memorable entrance : 「もし(明かりを消して床に伏せる

The bronze light was back on in his apartment, which seemed furnished in books. Books in various languages lined the walls and were stacked along the floor. His furniture was crates of more books, the stock left from a small Russian bookstore he'd opened then closed after receiving threats and a bomb in the mail. Above [5] his desk, he'd tracked a street map of Odessa, where he'd grown up beside the Black Sea. There were circles of red ink along a few of the streets. I didn't ask that night, but later, when I knew him better, I asked what the red circles marked.

"Good bakeries," he said. [10]

When the university didn't renew his contract, he moved away suddenly. It didn't surprise me. He'd been on the move since deserting to the British during the War. He'd lived in England, and Canada, and said he never knew where else was next, but that sooner or later staying in one place reminded him that where he [15] belonged no longer existed. He'd lived on Farwell, a street whose name sounded almost like saying goodbye.

Tonight, I jogged down Farwell to the lake, past the puddled tennis courts and the pier with its green beacon, and then along the empty beach. Waves were rushing in and I ran as if being [20] chased, tightroping along the foaming edge of water. My shoes peeled flying clods of footprints from the sand. It was late by the time I reached the building where I lived, the hallways quiet, supper smoke still ringing the lightbulbs. In the dark, my room with its windows raised smelled of wet screens and tangerines. [25]

代わりに)窓から顔を出していたら」という仮定が隠れている．もしそうしていたら，(それこそシャリアピンばりの)「堂々たる登場になっていたろうに」

I'm sorry I missed it： チャンスを逃して残念だ

[35] my nerves aren't what they should be： こうした表現を通して，ロシア系移民バボヴィッチのつらい過去が少しずつ浮き彫りにされていく．

[1] was back on： ふたたび点灯していた

seemed furnished in books： 部屋に備えつけてあるものはみな本でできているみたいに見えた

[3] crates： (運搬用の大きめの)木箱

[6] Odessa： ウクライナ南西部，黒海に面する港町．20 世紀初頭は革命の中心地で，エイゼンシュテインの映画でも知られる戦艦ポチョムキンの叛乱が起きたのもここ．第二次大戦で 2 年半にわたって，枢軸国側の激しい攻撃にさらされた．

[10] "Good bakeries"： かりにここが "Good bookshops" となっていたら，どれだけつまらない小説になるか．バボヴィッチの年齢からして，それら美味しいパン屋があったのはおそらく第二次大戦以前のことであり，それらのパン屋も，パン屋が象徴していた生活も，戦争によって破壊されてしまったにちがいない．

[12] desert(ing) to the British： (ソ連軍を)脱走してイギリス軍に逃げ込む

[14] said he never knew where else was next： つぎはいったいどこに行くのか見当もつかないと言っていた

but that sooner or later . . .： that は said からつなげて読む．

[15] that where he belonged no longer existed： この that 節の主語は where he belonged (自分が属している場所，故郷——要するに戦前のオデッサ)．

[16] Farwell, a street whose name sounded almost like saying goodbye： Farwell に e を加えれば Farewell (さようなら)．

[18] Tonight： 最初の段落と最後の段落が同じ言葉ではじまっている．ひとつの円環が閉じられたような印象．

puddled： 水たまりのできた．「雪」と「雨」の対比．

[21] tightroping： 綱渡りでもするように進みながら foam(ing)： 泡を立てる

[22] peel(ed)： ひきはがす

flying clods of footprints： 直訳すれば「宙に舞う足跡の塊」．濡れた砂が靴の裏にくっついてはがれる感じをよく伝えている．

[23] supper smoke still ringing the lightbulbs： 電球のまわりで輪になっている煙が，かりに秋刀魚の煙であっても不思議はない気がするほど，ダイベックの叙情は日本人にもしっくり来る．そういえば，一番最後のイメージも，日本の冬とは切っても切りはなせない tangerines (ミカン) の匂い．

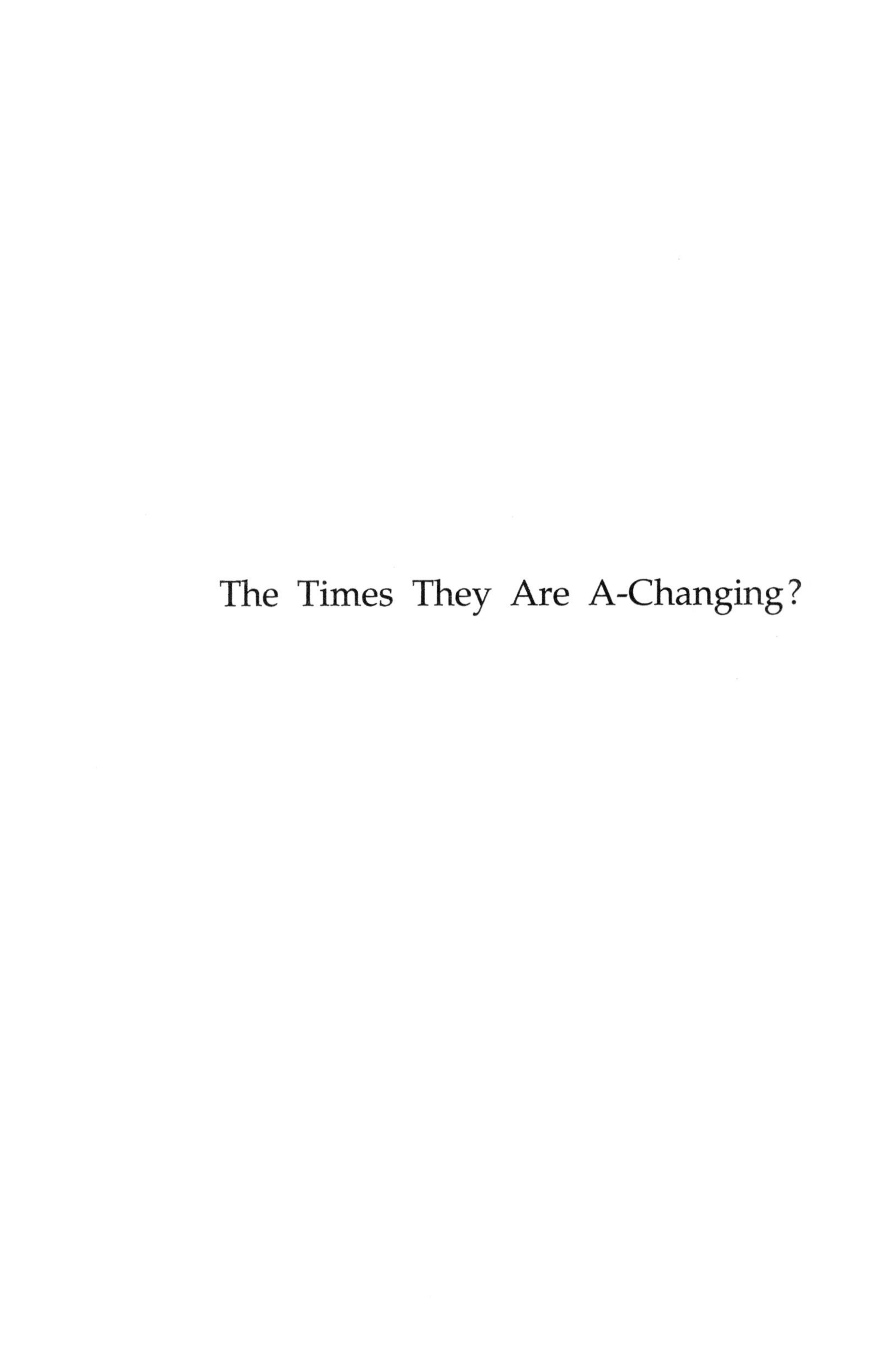

The Times They Are A-Changing?

Clean up after your dog

SESSION 7

Stupid Cross-dressing Killer Werewolves: America in the Late 20th Century

■

Jerry Griswold

IF YOU WANT to understand America today, where would you begin? You might, for example, go to the theater and watch movies Americans like to see. Why?

Movies are our shared dreams, the dream life of our culture. Up there on the big screen, you can see the themes and issues we [5] are struggling with. Sit in the theater like a psychiatrist. Ask yourself: What do you make of America near the end of the Twentieth Century?

I. Stupid Cross-dressing Killer Werewolves (or "Category Breakdown")

Take, for example, four films popular in the U.S. during the summer of 1994: [10]

Forrest Gump. In this film, Tom Hanks plays a "simpleminded" man with a low I.Q. In a very funny way, however, he turns out to be the most influential man in America during the last thirty years. For example: when he is a child, Forrest Gump wears braces on his legs and tries to dance for a guest at his mother's [15] boarding house, for a young man who plays the guitar; that guest

ジェリー・グリズウォルドはサンディエゴ州立大英文・比較文学科の人気教師．児童文学研究者として知られ，著書 *Audacious Kids: Coming of Age in America's Classsic Children's Books* は，阿吽社から『家なき子の物語』の邦題で訳が出た．同じ大学で教える奥さんの Linda はスペイン系だが，愛する国は日本で，アメリカの映画と大衆小説に見る日本イメージの変遷も，得意なテーマの 1 つにしている．趣味はサイクリング．夏になるとワシントン州からカリフォルニアまでの西海岸の走破を試みる．その途中，サイクリング専門誌の記事を仕上げてしまう仕事人でもある．㋚

[4] the dream life of our culture： 100 年前の成立期から映画のスクリーンには観客のファンタジーが投影されてきた．西部劇もメロドラマもオカルト映画もロード・ムービーも，ハリウッド映画はアメリカ文化の深層にうずまく夢の投影だった．

[7] What do you make of America： アメリカをどのように捉えるのか

[11] *Forrest Gump*： 題名は主人公の名前から．Gump は「ボケナス」に似た響きのある罵倒語だけど，Gumption（「ガッツ」の意味）の省略形としても使われる．フットボールのフの字も知らずに，フィールドをバカ走りしてしまう主人公にピッタリの名だ．

"simpleminded"： この言葉はほとんど「単純バカ」に近い軽蔑の響きをもつ．引用符を付けたことで「いかにも人がそう呼びそうな」というニュアンスが加わる．

[15] braces： フォレスト少年は足が悪く，体を支える固定装具が必要だった．その彼が突然超自然的な「走り」を見せる――という筋立てが現代人の支持を受けるだろうということは，同じ「障害者の特殊才能もの」の『レインマン』でも立証ずみ．

[16] boarding house： モーテル以前の時代には，旅人をまかない付きで泊める旅籠屋があった．

turns out to be Elvis Presley and, in this way, Elvis learns to swivel his hips when he performs on stage. Later, this "stupid" man invests money in the Apple Computer Company because he thinks they sell fruit, and he becomes a millionaire. *Forrest Gump* celebrates the wise fool. The distinctions between stupidity and [5] cleverness break down.

Mrs. Doubtfire. Robin Williams plays a character who is separated from his children by a divorce. To be near them, Williams' character disguises himself as a woman and is hired as their housekeeper. There are many funny moments in the film that are [10] the result of Williams' cross-dressing: when Mrs. Doubtfire is cooking, for example, he/she forgets about his/her stuffed bra and her/his "breasts" catch on fire. In *Mrs. Doubtfire,* like the movies *Tootsie* or *The Crying Game,* the distinctions between male and female break down. [15]

Serial Mom. Kathleen Turner plays an ideal suburban housewife who is a good cook and very concerned about her family's problems. She solves those problems by becoming a serial killer, by murdering people. When her son gets poor grades at school, she runs over his teacher with her car. When her daughter is dis- [20] appointed that a boy doesn't show up for a date, Mom finds him and stabs him. And when her dentist husband is bothered by a rude patient who wants work done on the weekend, she kills him, too. What's difficult to explain is that this is a very funny film. John Waters' film is like Morita's *The Family Game*. You don't [25] know whether to laugh. You keep asking yourself: "Is that meant to be funny?" *Serial Mom* is an example of "edge humor" where the distinctions between tragedy and comedy break down.

Wolf. Jack Nicholson plays a timid businessman who is bitten by a werewolf and becomes one himself. Most of the time, he in- [30] habits a world between his two identities. For example, when he encounters a business rival in the men's restroom, Nicholson's character urinates on the man's shoes and says, "I'm just marking my territory." Like *Beauty and the Beast* or *Splash* (where Darryl Hannah plays a mermaid), *Wolf* presents a character who is half- [35]

[1] in this way, Elvis learns to swivel his hips： ひざを落としてセクシーに腰を回すのはエルビスのトレードマーク．ちなみに *Back to the Future* には，チャック・ベリーが30年後の世界からやってきた少年のギター・ギグをもとにロックンロールを発明するというエピソードがありました．

[3] Apple Computer Company： ヒッピー文化の余韻の消えない70年代のカリフォルニアの倉庫で，2人のオタク青年が開発した，遊び感覚に徹した魔法の小箱がアップル1号機．以後，超大企業IBMを追い落とすほどの勢いで成長を続けたのは周知の通り．

[7] *Mrs. Doubtfire*： 邦題は『ミセス・ダウト』．ところでこの映画，演技(完璧な家事と子供の教育をこなす老家政婦)と現実(ダメ親父)との間の Category Breakdown は起こっているのだろうか？

[14] *Tootsie*： 女装のダスティン・ホフマンがレズっ気のある女優(ジェシカ・ラング)に惚れられる，1982年の社会派コメディー．邦題は『トッツィー』だが，英語の発音は [túːtsi]．

The Crying Game： 『クライング・ゲーム』．1992年度のイギリス映画の秀作．心優しきIRAの兵士と，彼みずからが誘拐した英国黒人兵士との間に生まれる人間的な心の通い合いの映画かと思ってみていると，捕虜の青年はあっさり死んでしまい，あとは．．．いや，書かないのがこれから見る人への礼儀だろう．この2作に，ぼくとしては是非クローネンバーグ監督の『M・バタフライ』を加えたい．

[18] solves those problems： 家族の誰かに小さな問題が起こり，そのゴタゴタが20分か25分の放映時間の間にパパとママのユーモアあふれる思いやりによって解決をみる，というのが往年のアメリカン・ホームドラマの典型的パターン．この映画はそれの法外なパロディーにもなっている．

[25] John Waters： アメリカ的な趣味の悪さ，下品さを全部かき集めた『ピンク・フラミンゴ』『フィメール・トラブル』などの作品で「トラッシュの帝王」の名をほしいままにした彼も，『ヘアスプレー』以降はメインストリームを歩む．

Morita's *The Family Game*： 森田芳光監督『家族ゲーム』(1983)

[33] marking my territory： 犬が電柱におしっこをするのは，「縄張り本能」のためと言われています．

[34] *Beauty and the Beast*： ルイ王朝期に書かれたお伽話を，1946年，詩人ジャン・コクトーが映画化した不朽の名作．野獣のような姿をした悪魔のもとに通うことを条件に彼の魔法で病の父の命を救ってもらった美女が，野獣の面の下に人間的な魂を見いだしていく物語は超有名．ジェリーはこのテーマに入れ込んでいて，『ノートルダムのせむし男』から『ザ・フライ』に至る百近いバリエーションをインプット，パソコンを駆使して，教育用CD–ROMを作り上げた．

human. The distinctions between human and animal break down.

Okay, these are enough examples to suggest what you might see if you sat in an American theater during the summer of 1994 and watched our collective dreams. What do you see? That "Teenage Mutant Ninja Turtles" have been replaced by "Stupid Cross-Dressing Killer Werewolves"? That's not quite it. What may already be apparent is that you frequently see a condition that can be described as "category breakdown" — a twilight world where distinctions are beginning to disintegrate, where opposites begin to intermingle: wise and foolish, male and female, adult and child, gay and straight, tragic and comic, animal and human. Where does that "category breakdown" come from? And why is it so prevalent in our time?

II. There Will Never Be Another Woodstock Nation (or Halfway to a Postfigurative Culture)

Several years ago, I was in the "red light district" or "willow quarter" in Amsterdam and I happened to meet Margaret Mead, the great anthropologist. (I hasten to add that we were both there for anthropological reasons.) I was happy to have that chance meeting because it gave me the opportunity to tell her how much her book *Culture and Commitment* meant to me.

In that book, Mead says there are three kinds of cultures. *Prefigurative cultures* where lifestyles are determined by tradition: "My grandfather made canoes. My father made canoes. I make canoes." *Cofigurative cultures* where lifestyles are determined by one's peers: "All my friends are wearing black leather jackets and blue jeans. I wear a black leather jacket and blue jeans." And *Postfigurative cultures* where an individual doesn't follow any particular pattern but determines his or her own lifestyle: "I'm doing my own thing."

[3] Okay: この文章はクラスでしゃべっている様子をそのまま再現したのに近いスタイルになっている．この "Okay" も，話を次に進めようとするときのきまり文句．

[5] That: (Do you see) that . . .

"Teenage Mutant Ninja Turtles": 最初コミックとして登場 (1984–)，次にテレビ・アニメ (1987–)，そして映画連作 (1990–) とアメリカではバカウケしている忍者亀シリーズ．Mutant といえば SF，Ninja といえば東洋アクション，Turtles で動物アニメと，相場が決まっていた．Teenage で連想される爽快青春ものを含め，このタイトルには，それら各ジャンルを強く連想させる言葉をごたまぜにした趣がある．

[7] That's not quite it: 「それだけでは言い尽くしていない」．"That's it" は「ズバリその通り」．

[9] twilight: 1960年代初頭の SF 怪奇テレビ・シリーズ *Twilight Zone* の邦題「ミステリー・ゾーン」は，正確な意訳だけれど，twilight のもともとの意味は「光と闇の入り交じった薄明状態」．ここでは白黒の決まらない世界の形容となっている．

[15] red light district: 日本の「赤線」の語源は警察の地図に引かれた赤い線だが，こちらの表現は売春宿の入口の赤い灯火に由来する．"willow quarter" は日本語の「柳町」を英語に直訳したもの．

[16] Margaret Mead: 「女流」という言葉が生き生きしていた20世紀中葉の代表的女流文化人．彼女の人柄と精力的な活動ぶりを知りたい人は，ぜひ娘 Mary Catherine Bateson による伝記『娘の眼から』(国文社) をお読みください．

[18] chance meeting: この chance は形容詞．

[20] *Culture and Commitment*: ジェネレーション・ギャップということが盛んにいわれた1970年の本．邦題『地球時代の文化論』．

[25] peers: people who are equal in rank or age

black leather jackets and blue jeans: 「ブルー・ジーンと皮ジャンパー」というアダモの歌がありました．この格好でオートバイを乗り回す，というのがマーロン・ブランドが若かった頃の「反抗的な」――すなわち「クール」な――ライフスタイル．

These distinctions do more than offer a way to understand different cultures in different regions. They also provide a way of understanding how cultures change over time — especially American culture.

From its beginnings to the early part of the nineteenth century, [5] much of American culture was prefigurative. Tradition counted and if your ancestors were farmers, for example, chances were very good that you and your offspring would be farmers, too. The nineteenth century marked a period of transition. Tradition and parents were no longer such powerful forces. The Industrial [10] Revolution took young men and women off the farm and sent them to the city where they took up unprecedented occupations. The waves of immigrants who came to America and those who headed west to settle the frontier were largely individuals who broke with their parents and with their past. Prefigurative culture [15] was breaking down.

The Twentieth Century saw the rise of a cofigurative culture, where lifestyles are determined by peers. In the 1920's and 1930's, for example, there were "flappers" and that lifestyle pictured in Fitzgerald's *The Great Gatsby*. Before and during World War II, [20] there was the Swing Era where a whole generation of young Americans danced to Benny Goodman while dressed in their zoot suits or, later, in their uniform soldiers' uniforms. Later still, in the 1950's and the Eisenhower era, conformity became a kind of national passion with everyone trying to blend in, live in a subur- [25] ban tract home , and have a life like that on the television program *Ozzie and Harriet*. Those who didn't want to be conformists could find their peers by becoming beatniks or by rebelling along the lines of "angry young men" like James Dean or Marlon Brando. [30]

It seems to me that our cofigurative culture peaked in the 1960's and 1970's when the bland conformity of the Kennedy years gave way to the era of Woodstock and the Counterculture. Then, it seemed, nearly everyone of a certain generation dressed in certain ways, shared similar values, and rebelled against those who [35]

[6] counted: was important

[7] chances were very good that . . . : ～の可能性は高かった.

[9] mark(ed) a period of transition: ちょうど移行期にあたる

[10] The Industrial Revolution: 産業革命, 鉄道敷設, 西部開拓 . . . みな南北戦争(1861–65)を境に急展開を見た現象. ヨーロッパの貧農の流入の最盛期は1880年代からの30年あまり.

[19] flappers: 短い「ボブ・ヘアー」にショート・スカートのハデハデ娘. 彼女らに影響されて大正末年から昭和初期に東京のカフエ(カフェじゃなく)に現われたのが「モガ」(モダン・ガール).

that lifestyle pictured in Fitzgerald's *The Great Gatsby*: フィッツジェラルドが29歳のときに出版されたこの小説には, 中西部の田舎から出てきてまたたくまに財を築いた青年が, 毎晩のようにパーティーを開き, そこに最先端のファッションできめた男女が集まったようすが生き生きと書かれている.

[21] the Swing Era: スイングの時代といえば1930年代. swing jazz の音楽的定義は曖昧で, 要するにリズムが「ごきげん」ならスイングだったといってよい. 白人の Benny Goodman の登場で,「ふつうの若者」に浸透.

[22] zoot suits: 映画『マルコム X』でおなじみになった, ダボダボ・スーツ. 1940年代の反抗的な黒人やメキシコ系の若者が着はじめたストリート・ファッションで, キャブ・キャロウェイらの黒人映画スターを通して広まった.

[24] conformity: 冷戦時代のイデオロギー的な締めつけの中で保守化した, 50年代 Silent Generation の, 物質経済繁栄の中での画一的順応主義の生活.

[25] suburban tract home: 50年代は, 都市の中流層が郊外の均質的な建て売り住宅に「大移動」した時期である.

[27] *Ozzie and Harriet*: 『陽気なネルソン』の邦題でやっていたネルソン家の生活ぶりは,『パパは何でも知っている』(*Father Knows Best*) のアンダーソン家の生活とともに, 日本中年族のアメリカへの憧憬の原形をつくっている.

[28] beatnik(s): Beat Generation の詩や小説にひかれて, 都市のボヘミアン生活を選んで生きる若者たち. 1958, 9年ころ急増.

[29] "angry young men": ロックンロールの始動期に, マーロン・ブランド主演の『乱暴者(あばれもの)』(1953) とジェームス・ディーン主演の『理由なき反抗』(1955) が, 怒れる(または鬱屈した)若者像を魅力的に演出している.

[35] shared similar values: 彼らの価値観のうちの数例——① 科学とテクノロジーは悪である, ② 警察はファシストの豚である, ③ セックス・ドラッグ・ロックンロールは人間性を解放する. (これはもちろん戯画的な説明です.)

against those who weren't their peers: この態度は "Don't trust anyone over thirty" (「30歳以上は信用するな」) というスローガンに集約される.

weren't their peers . It was a huge Movement because there were so many peers to share it with. "Baby Boomers," those born after World War II, constituted one third of America's population.

In the time which has followed, it seems to me, we have witnessed a gradual disintegration of a cofigurative culture. And we [5] are beginning to see a gradual transition to a postfigurative culture where patternless individuality will predominate. At the moment, however, we are in a transitional phase between these two states.

Take Youth Culture. While it may sadden Baby Boomers to [10] hear this, there may never be anything like the huge Youth Movement of the 60's and 70's, the Woodstock Nation, the Counterculture. Instead, in the 1980's and 1990's, what we have seen are mini-movements: punks, preppies, grunge, retro, etc. Mini-movements are halfway houses in the move from uniform peer [15] cultures to category-less individuality.

This same phenomena can be seen in the way people identify themselves. There was a time, through the 1950's, when people readily described themselves as "Americans." This "assimilationist" urge was so strong that many who felt they were outside [20] the main culture tried to "fit in." So, for example, a Mexican-American citizen named "Ernesto" might have adopted the more English-sounding name of "Ernest" and asked his friends to call him "Ernie." At the same time, the major culture made moves to bring in everyone that they felt were outsiders. During this time, [25] for example, there was a great movement to end racial separation and to integrate schools so that black and white students could study together. The point is that many wanted to be the same thing, the same kind of American.

Now, our cofigurative culture is breaking down and slowly [30] giving way to a postfigurative one. In this intermediate situation, this halfway state, what we now see are micro-identities or new forms of tribalism. Now, Americans are more likely to identify themselves as gay, women, African-Americans, Asian-Americans, Mexican-Americans, Irish-Americans, and so forth. You can [35]

[1] Movement: 大文字になっているのは，世代全体が実際「一つの」運動を展開していた(感じがする)から．

[2] "Baby Boomers": 日本で「団塊世代」というと，1946–50年くらいまでに生まれた比較的狭い範囲を言うが，アメリカのベビー・ブーマーはもっと広く1950年代生まれ全体を含むことも多い．60年代以降に生まれたものは，これに対し，"Generation X"という名が定着した．

[10] Take . . . : Take, for example, . . .

[12] Woodstock Nation: ジェリーがこの原稿を書いたのは1994年秋．その年8月に *Woodstock 94* が開かれた．25年前の神話的フェスティバルの現役組を含め，たくさんのスターが参加したが，かつて「ウッドストック共和国」を夢見た世代にとって，「ただの大きな商業的催しもの」という印象は避けがたかった．

[14] punks: 登場したのは76年ロンドン．Sex Pistols, The Clashら労働者階級のpunk rockersの爆発的な人気とともに，アメリカにもpunk sceneが飛び火したが，こちらでは階級的な怒りの表現とはなりえなかった．

preppies: Punksとは逆に伝統的価値観への順応を表現するファッションの実践者．50年代の裕福な大学生の格好にならって，カシミアのセーターやタータン・チェックのスカートを着用．「何をどの店で買うか」が意味をもった．

grunge: 90年代初頭にシアトル中心に盛り上がったインディー系の放埒で荒々しいgrunge rock (Nirvana, Pearl Jam 等) を支持する若者層が好んで着た，薄汚さを演出するファッション．

retro: 特に60～70年代ファッションへの回帰現象をさしている．

[19] "assimilationist" urge: 主流文化へ溶け込んでいこうとする衝動．

[24] made moves: 働きかけをした

[26] there was a great movement to end racial separation . . . : ジェリーと同年代のポール・アルケビュランがこの動きに対してどう反応したかは，34ページ後半以降を読んで下さい．

[32] micro-identities: 次の文に説明されている．「オタク化現象」も，その最たるものと考えてよいかもしれない．

[33] tribalism: 同族意識; 小さな「部族」(tribes) に分かれる傾向．

see the same situation in the rise of ethnic literary works, for example, or in the appearance of movies (*Malcolm X, The Joy Luck Club, Like Water for Chocolate,* etc.) that speak to or about these segments of the population.

In other words, in this transition to the patternless individuality [5] of a postfigurative culture, what we see are temporary solutions: the breakup of large cultural movements into mini-movements, the breakup of large social units into micro-identities. What we see, in other words, is another form of "category breakdown." [10]

Of course, this is just what we noticed when we entered the movie theater and watched America's collective dreams projected on to the big screen. Now we can see that these films are symptoms of large cultural forces at work in America in the late Twentieth Century. In the American fascination with cross-dressing, [15] werewolves, "edge humor," and the wise fool, we also see this gradual disintegration of categories.

This condition is not a failure of nerve or a symptom of decline, as critics on the Right would say. Instead, it is a reflection of the fact that we are at an intermediate phase. America has not yet [20] arrived at the condition of a postfigurative culture — that fluid state of category-less or pattern-less individuality.

III. News Bulletin: White Boys Wearing Dreadlocks! (or The End of Trends)

"But," I hear you say, "can this postfigurative culture (this culture of individuals) be called a 'culture' at all?" In truth, what a postfigurative culture implies is not the end of culture, but the [25] end of trends.

Let me explain myself by way of anecdote. Last week, MTV issued a news bulletin, a fashion note: "White boys wearing dreadlocks!" Musicians in two groups, "Counting Crows" and "Big Mountain," have started wearing their hair in dreadlocks — [30]

[2] *Malcolm X*: ラップ文化の隆盛で，これはいけるとにらんだハリウッドが，『ドゥ・ザ・ライト・シング』(1989) でメジャー入りしたスパイク・リー監督を起用して制作した 1992 年の作品．この映画のヒットは日本でもマルコム・ブームを呼び，彼の顔をあしらった T シャツを陽気に着込んだ六本木のヒップホップ少年が，在日黒人の怒りを買ったのは記憶に新しい．

The Joy Luck Club: 中国系アメリカ人家族を描いたエイミー・タンの小説の映画化 (1993).

[3] *Like Water for Chocolate*: 1900 年代のメキシコの一家族の生き様を女たちの視点から描いた魔術的リアリズムの傑作．メキシコの小説家エキヴァルの同名の小説の映画化 (1993)．外国映画を見るのは苦手なアメリカでも話題を呼び，同じ頃アメリカでもよく読まれた Banana Yoshimoto の *Kitchen* とペアで語られたりもした．

[19] critics on the Right: 「右」よりの批評家は，当然ながら「昔はよかった」という言説をくり出す．たとえばシカゴ大学アラン・ブルーム教授の『アメリカン・マインドの終焉』*The Closing of the American Mind* (1993) は，現代の政治的・社会的危機が知的没落に起因するものであると説き，「ちかごろのアメリカ」を嘆く人々の間で大きな反響を得た．

[21] fluid: flowing like a liquid; very changeable

[27] explain myself: 釈明する

MTV: ケーブルテレビ局としてビデオ・クリップの 24 時間放映を始めたのが 1981 年．80 年代以降のポップ音楽を語るなら，これを見ないとしょうがない．

that style of long, braided and frizzed hair, made popular by Bob Marley and Rastafarians. They started sporting this hairstyle a few months ago. The implication of this style bulletin was that other fashionable caucasians may soon be doing the same. Having been identified by MTV, this whole trend may be over in six [5] months. My point is how, in this age of electronic media and immediacy, this mini-trend occurred in so short a time. A decade or so ago, this trend might have lasted for two or three years. Now, electronic bulletins are flashed from the frontline, categorized as a trend, and (having been identified) rendered passé. [10]

Now, if you want to see what the future will be like, imagine that this trend had occurred not in six *months* but in six *weeks* — or even six days. A trend starts, word is flashed out on the computer networks, and it dies. In the future, when electronic communication is nearly instantaneous, "originality" will only last for a few [15] moments. Eventually, it will become virtually impossible, unimportant, and obsolete.

At that moment, we will witness the death of the "avant garde," the disappearance of trends, and an end to the frenetic obligation or desire to "keep up" or "stay ahead." In these cir- [20] cumstances, today's exhausted participants in the "rat race" might issue a collective sigh of relief. But more importantly, with the end of trends, we begin to witness the birth of postfigurative culture. But what kind of "culture"?

We might begin to frame an answer by noting that, these days, [25] the most common method of composing music is a technique called "sampling." Sitting at a computer, a composer can take snatches of music from here and there, slightly alter them, add them to others and come up with a piece of music. Of course, I realize that the word "composer" may be an obsolete term here; [30] perhaps "combiner" would be more accurate. In any event, with sampling the whole notion of "originality" goes out the window and the notion of "copyright" seems an anachronism.

In a fashion, this situation resembles that of the late Middle Ages. As T. S. Eliot suggests in his great essay "Tradition and In- [35]

[1] long, braided and frizzed : 白人や黄色人種が「レゲエ頭」にするには，長く伸ばした髪を細く束ねてチリヂリにする必要がある．

Bob Marley and Rastafarians : Rastafarians とは，アフリカ帰還の願望に強く裏打ちされたアフリカ系ジャマイカ人の宗教信徒で，ラス・タファリ家のエチオピア皇帝ハイレ・セラシエを，いつかカリブと新大陸の同胞を母なる大陸に連れ帰る神の化身として奉じる．白人士官が土地の女に生ませた Bob は 16 歳でこの信徒となり，以後，民族主義的メッセージの濃い歌をレゲエのリズムに乗せて歌うようになった．

[4] caucasian(s) : [kɔːkéiʒən] 白色人種

Having been identified by MTV : 「MTV が注目した動きであるから」．MTV 的世界でのトレンドは短い．identify するとは，ここでは，それまで誰も気にとめていなかった現象を切り出して示すこと．

[6] immediacy : media が媒体，すなわち介在するものだとすれば，その media が打ち払われた状態が immediacy だ．「media は immediacy に向かう」ということは，手紙 → 電信 → 電話 → テレビ電話，という進化の過程を考えれば明らかだろう．

[9] the frontline : （ファッションの）最前線

[10] (are) rendered passé: become outdated; are no longer fashionable.

[19] frenetic : busy to the point of being crazy

[20] "keep up" or "stay ahead" : そういえば，「あの人，すすんでる」という日本語を最近あまり聞かなくなった．「おしゃれ」は現在必ずしも流行の先端を意味しない．

[21] "rat race" : 仕事社会の激烈な競争をいうフレーズが，ここではカッコヨサをめぐる競争に使われている．

[22] issue a collective sigh of relief : みんなして一斉に安堵の溜息をつく

[29] and come up with a piece of music : 「それで一曲でき上がり」

[31] In any event : in any case

with sampling : サンプリングの登場によって

[32] goes out the window : 日本語の「吹きとんでしまう」よりイメージが具体的ですね．

[34] In a fashion : in a way, in a sense

[35] T. S. Eliot : 『荒地』(1922) の詩人は，のちに大文芸批評家となりました．

dividual Talent," Dante was not trying to be "original" when he wrote his masterpiece *The Divine Comedy*. Instead, Dante was "syncretistic." He borrowed from various schools of philosophy and theology, from literature, from history, from his own life, and he wove all this together into an impressive whole or summary. [5] He "sampled" and created his own thing.

Today, in bars in Tokyo or America's cities or elsewhere on the planet, you can see another kind of "sampling." You can see an extraordinary kind of eclecticism. In places that almost seem a premonition of the bar scene in *Star Wars*, you will see: people [10] wearing t-shirts that celebrate Nelson Mandela, Amazon's rain forests, or gay pride at UCLA. On the tables are Corona beers or Heineken or Kirin. On the walls are pictures of Bob Marley, Sylvester Stallone, and Brigitte Bardot. In the background you hear the sounds of the Rolling Stones, Roy Orbison, and Abba. On [15] the televisions are pictures of Michael Jackson waving goodbye in Los Angeles, a soccer game in Birmingham, and a concert at a Buddhist temple in Nara where Bob Dylan shares the stage with Yoshiki.

Call this "global culture," or even "*kokusai-ka*" [international- [20] ization], and you don't quite describe it. Instead, you see "sampling." You see the rise of a postfigurative culture where individuals make their own unities out of the fragments left over from "category breakdown." In other words, in 1994, we are halfway between the peer-determined trendiness of a cofigurative [25] culture and the eclectic individuality of a postfigurative culture. What we can begin to glimpse on the horizon is the rise of a new transnational and pluralistic personality — a condition where we may be able to echo (or "sample") the poet Walt Whitman and say: "I contain multitudes." [30]

[3] "syncretistic": syncretismのもともとの意味は「神仏混交」のような宗教的混交主義.

[9] eclecticism: 折衷主義; 折衷の精神でつくられたもの

[10] premonition of the bar scene in *Star Wars*: どのような意味で「スター・ウォーズ」の世界を先取りしているかは, 次に列挙される.

[12] Corona beers or Heineken or Kirin: それぞれメキシコ, オランダ, 日本のビール.

[13] ... Bob Marley, Sylvester Stallone, and Brigitte Bardot: 70年代ジャマイカと80年代アメリカと60年代フランスとが混在しつつ, 常に今ここにあるということ.

[15] Roy Orbison: 60年代前半の "Crying" や "Oh, Pretty Woman" のヒットで知られる. 1988年に急逝. 晩年に収録したk. d. langとのデュエットは感涙もの. Abba: 70年代に世界を席巻したスウェーデン出身の4人組. あまりの売れ方に, 以後しばらく, ちょっと恥ずかしい存在に甘んじていたけれど, 95年のオーストラリアのゲイ映画『プリシラ』などによって「復活」がうたわれている.

[17] a Buddhist temple in Nara: 1994年, 奈良東大寺で開かれたユネスコ主催の音楽フェスに, 当時日本に短期滞在中のジェリーは出かけて行っている.

[19] Yoshiki: 妖艶なるニッポンのロッカー, Xのあの YOSHIKI.

[21] and you don't quite describe it: (そう呼んでも)言いつくせてはいない

[26] eclectic individuality: 好きなものを寄せ集めて「自分」をつくること.

[28] transnational and pluralistic personality: 「国民性」の枠を超えていろいろな要素が混ざりあった人格. 1950年生まれの中流白人のアメリカ人よりも, 1970年生まれの方が, その性格のなかに「世代」にも「国民性」にもしばられない部分が大きいことは事実のようです.

[30] "I contain multitudes": アメリカの国民詩人ホイットマンの超有名な長詩 *Leaves of the Grass* の中の言葉. 多人種・多民族の寄り合い所帯であるアメリカという国では「人種のるつぼ」の神話に代表されるような, 「多からの一」のビジョンがごく最近まで国民的な理想となっていた. その意味ではリベラルな雰囲気をもつジェリーのこのエッセイも, このエンディングでは, アメリカの心の琴線にふれる種類の伝統的理想主義に傾いている, といえそうだ.

SESSION 8

Lessons Learned at School

■

Joanne Elbinger Higashi

MENTION "JAPANESE SCHOOLS" and many Westerners imagine immaculately-groomed second-graders tackling trigonometry in groups that work together like parts of a clock. A smiling, dedicated teacher stands nearby.

Or they see exhausted students, trudging to school after studying all night for entrance exams. Their stomachs churn — "What if my hair is a millimeter too long? My socks the wrong shade of white?" But they'd better hurry! A minute late and they could be crushed in the gates. [5]

Of course I have found Japanese schools to be neither genius factories nor prisons. But I did find many surprises in the three public Japanese elementaries — one in rural Mie Prefecture and two in Tokyo — that my two boys have attended. [10]

The assumptions made at these schools fascinate me because they seem to influence children more reliably than explicit teachings. [15]

My son's After-school Care teacher once told me about the day some children saw him munching a hunk of raw carrot from his lunch box.

"How can you eat that?" they asked in shock and disgust. [20]

"What do you mean?" my amused son replied. "It's sweet!"

The staff began giving the curious children snacks of raw veg-

ジョアン・エルビンガー・東さんは，ナイト・リッダー・ファイナンシャル・ニュース特派員などを経て，現在はNHKや新聞の翻訳者．今回は，日本の学校教育について率直な体験記を書いてもらった．●

[2] immaculately-groomed : 完璧な身だしなみの
tackling : tackle は問題などに「取り組む」
[3] trigonometry : 三角法
[4] dedicated : 献身的な
[5] exhausted : tired out
trudging : trudge は「とぼとぼ歩く」
[6] Their stomachs churn : (心配で)胃が重くなる，気が重くなる
[7] the wrong shade of white : (同じ白でも)間違った色合いの白
[8] A minute late and they could be crushed in the gates : という事件が本当にあったことは，まだ記憶に新しい．
[12] elementaries : 小学校
[14] assumptions : (物事を考えたり行なったりする上での)前提
[15] explicit : はっきり表に出た
[17] After-school Care : 学童保育
[18] munching a hunk of raw carrot : 「生の人参を丸ごともぐもぐ食べている」. munch に関する『ジーニアス英和辞典』の絶妙の説明は，「(. . . を)(口を閉じたまままいかにも楽しそうに)むしゃむしゃ [もぐもぐ] 食べる」

etables and were amazed that the children learned to enjoy them.

Throughout Japan, especially in cartoons and children's books, it is assumed that children detest vegetables. A favorite topic of health officials and parenting magazines is, "How to sneak vegetables down your child's throat." [5]

Where I grew up, eating sticks of raw carrot, celery and cucumber was commonplace and I assumed my own children would like vegetables. In fact, they've been known to fight over a stalk of celery or a carrot.

There are some Japanese assumptions that we might do well to [10] adopt in the U.S.: that any child can learn through persistent effort; that parents will stay together and support their children's education, that children will follow directions and cooperate in a group.

Although I try not to pass judgment on Japanese ways, my ob- [15] jectivity breaks down when I consider the assumption that government authorities need no parental input in order to run the schools.

Not only do Japanese educational authorities not actively seek parents' opinions, but even parents who try to give feedback have [20] a hard time finding a channel through which they can make themselves heard.

Boards of education are not elected by the public or responsible to voters. Japanese taxpayers are even denied access to information about the school system to which they commit money, time [25] and their own children.

In America, it is parents' job to tell school officials what we want for our children, and part of their job to listen. The Parent-Teacher Association (PTA) was created to facilitate communication between parents and schools. [30]

In Japan, many parents and educators have told me that schools prefer to hide problems rather than confront them. Parents often say their children are "held hostage," because teachers have the power to write a negative report that can prevent their child from getting into a prestigious school, which will presum- [35]

[3] detest: to hate; dislike

[4] How to sneak . . . your child's throat: 「こっそり入れる」. ハンバーグに混ぜるとか, ケーキに混ぜるとか, 一連のコソクな手段.

[8] fight over: ～を取り合いする

[10] might do well to adopt: 見習っていい

[11] through persistent effort: 粘り強く頑張れば

[13] directions: 言われたこと, 指示

[15] my objectivity breaks down: 「私の客観性は崩れる」. 主観を持ち込まずにはいられないということ.

[17] parental input: 親からの意見

[19] Not only do . . . authorities not actively seek parents' opinions: not が2つあるのでややこしいが, 「日本の教育者は親の意見を積極的に求めないだけではなく . . .」

[20] feedback: (情報・サービスなどの受け手の側からの)感想. 17行目の input と同じく, 電子工学・情報理論の用語が一般化した例.

[21] channel: 経路

[23] Boards of education: 教育委員会

[25] commit: 預ける, 任せる

[29] facilitate: to make easy; help

[33] are "held hostage": 人質に取られている

[35] a prestigious school: 一流校

presumably: 「恐らくは」. 世間ではみなそう思っているようだが, というニュアンス.

ably limit their chances of getting a desirable job.

The strong, underlying assumption is *shikata ga nai,* or "there is nothing we can do about it."

I began to discover this when I moved to Tokyo in 1991. I learned that my first-grader's new teacher, Yamamoto Sensei, [5] warned the mothers at their first meeting that she sometimes hits students. My son said she also kicked when really angry. Both boys said they often saw other teachers at N Elementary in Nerima Ward, on the playground and in the halls, knocking students on the head. [10]

In the tiny school my children attended in Mie, there was no such violence, and I never encountered it during my own 12 years of schooling. The idea of teacher striking student — particularly on the head — was as incongruous to me as the idea of walking across tatami in shoes. [15]

A few mothers said that since the teacher doesn't hit girls, it was not their problem.

I didn't care who got hit, or that my son said it didn't hurt. My concern was that small children look up to teachers as models of adult behavior. "When angry, punch," and "Resolve disagree- [20] ments with force," was not the education I wanted for anyone who lives on the same overcrowded train line as I do. After all, most will be bigger than me someday.

Several mothers agreed the teacher should not be hitting six-year-olds. But they all feared that their child might become a tar- [25] get if they objected.

I was incredulous. Teachers are public employees, what Americans call "civil servants" because our taxes pay their salaries and their job is to serve us. If need be, we can always go to higher authorities. [30]

The mothers laughed heartily at that, explaining that the principal's first priority was to avoid trouble in his last year before retirement. The Nerima board of education is composed of ward employees who rotate out every four or eight years. The mothers said most place a premium on gliding through [35]

[2] underlying assumption : 「ふだんは意識されない，隠れた前提」という意味の定型句.

[5] my first-grader('s) : 私の 1 年生の子供

[14] incongruous : 調和しない，不釣り合いな

[20] Resolve : 解決する

[31] laughed heartily at that : that は前段落の「私」の発言を指す.

[32] priority : 優先事項

[34] ward employees : 区役所の職員
rotate out : 交代する，持ち回りで務める

[35] place a premium on gliding through without incident : 事故なしに無事任期を務めることを重視する (place は動詞)

without incident.

Besides, they said, criticizing the government is too risky, and the school is an arm of the government. They called the government *okami*, a word that originally meant "upper part" and has come to also mean "emperor" or "master."

This is when I learned about my own assumptions. I was taught to revere democracy, meaning what the word's Greek origins imply: *demos* — "the people," *kratein* — "rule." We were also taught that we have not only the right to correct or reject government that fails to serve us, but the duty to do so.

I spent as much time as anyone in history class drawing cartoons and test-flying paper airplanes, so I was surprised to find that I took seriously the lofty words that floated only loosely in my memory.

Like most humans, I prefer to leave anything resembling political action to those who enjoy it. But in this case no one else was volunteering, and since corporal punishment is already officially forbidden, I thought it shouldn't be too hard to get it stopped.

Yamamoto Sensei herself said she did not like hitting children, but knew of no other way to control them when they refuse to listen.

I asked the head teacher to show her other ways.

Several months later, my son said, "She stopped hitting *me*, but she still hits other kids."

Head Teacher said the teachers' union would not allow teachers to be disciplined unless they cause serious injury or death. She recommended I talk to the principal.

At first the principal thought I had come because a few days earlier a teacher's beating had raised a welt on a child's head. Actually, I hadn't heard about that until he mentioned it. All he would say about Yamamoto Sensei was, "She told me she doesn't hit."

I asked the board of education if there was a way to stop teacher violence and was told, "We'll look into it and get back to you." Four months later I asked again and heard, "The person

[7] revere : to respect deeply

[11] I spent as much time as anyone in history class . . . : 歴史の時間に～したのは私もみんなと同じ

[13] the lofty words that floated . . . in my memory : 私の記憶にぼんやり漂っていたにすぎないはずの，（前の段落で述べられているような）高尚な言葉

[17] corporal punishment : 体罰

[22] the head teacher : 教頭

[25] would not allow teachers to be disciplined : 教師に注意や勧告を与えるのを許さない

[29] welt : みみずばれ

[34] get back to . . . : （特に電話で）「～にまた連絡する」. *She's promised to get back to me as soon as she hears any more news from the hospital.*

you spoke with earlier is gone now. We'll look into it and get back to you."

When I moved from Nerima five months later I had yet to hear from them.

Meanwhile I learned from a number of Japanese parents and educators that *genkotsu* — striking the head with the knuckles — is a common form of discipline viewed much like spanking in the West. Some parents even request that teachers punish their children physically, partly as a sign of complete trust in the teacher's authority, and partly to show humility, i.e., "My child is so backward, he may need a knock on the head to help him understand."

Coincidentally I learned that the prohibition against corporal punishment was effected in 1947, while Japan was under U.S. rule. So it did not necessarily reflect the will of the Japanese people.

American logic told me that if the majority of Japanese approve of corporal punishment, I should put up with it or send my children to private school. If the majority disapprove, the ban should be enforced.

At the next "Parents' Discussion," I asked for opinions.

Silence.

Fidgeting.

Some mothers explained afterward that "discussions" are generally directed by the teacher. They were not the place for a parent to raise an issue without prior approval, or to express an opinion that might contradict the teacher's.

One mother said, "We don't have a tradition of public discussion."

An educator explained, "In Japan, to openly disagree with someone is tantamount to rejecting their whole person. We can't separate the opinion from the person."

I proposed to the PTA president that we conduct an anonymous survey about teacher violence.

He said that surveys must be approved by the school, and added, "Our PTA is school-led. We cannot act independently."

[3] I had yet to hear from them : have yet to は「まだ～していない」

[7] spank(ing) : 尻をたたく

[10] backward : 憶えの悪い，発達の遅れた

[12] Coincidentally : by chance

[18] the ban should be enforced : (体罰の)禁止を守らせるべきである

[22] Fidget(ing) : そわそわしたしぐさをする

[25] without prior approval : 「前もって了承を取らずに」．悪名高き *nemawashi* がここでも必要ということか．

[26] contradict : to disagree with; be opposed to

[29] In Japan, to openly disagree with someone is tantamount to . . . : tantamount は「～に等しい」．日本をことさら卑下するつもりはないが，ひとつの意見に対する批判を全人格的攻撃と受け取られて(受け取って ?)しまうことは本当に多い．

[32] an anonymous survey : 無記名のアンケート

He killed my proposal without letting me bring it to the floor.

My intention here is not to depict Japanese education as mean or sinister. In fact, my dominant image of a Japanese elementary school is one abundant with joy and the warmth of camaraderie.

I strongly suspect that even as schools deny the existence of [5] teacher violence, many are quietly working to reduce it. It should help that this year the Ministry of Justice designated civil liberties commissioners empowered to investigate violence against children.

Once *okami* decides that *genkotsu* no longer belongs in Japanese [10] schools, I'm sure it will be eradicated much quicker than guns will be from American schools.

What worries me more about my experience in Nerima is the authorities' autocratic attitude and parents' meek acceptance of it. There appears to be little understanding that democracy entails [15] more than simply electing legislators.

It could well be that the Japanese prefer their system as is: assumption of the power of self-government inevitably comes with an assumption of responsibility.

And while decision by consensus feels unbearably slow to impatient [20] Americans, it is probably worth the wait for most Japanese, since few share Westerners' love of a "good argument."

If Japanese people do decide to start taking charge, however, I think they will have to start training the nation's future voters to instruct and oversee their government. [25]

In sixth grade in America I was assigned to research an issue and write my opinion to a congressperson. My fourth-grader in Japan was given a printed worksheet and instructed to choose an "opinion" from among several options. At the top was a space for the teacher to mark his "opinion" right or wrong! [30]

[1] bring it to the floor : 議題として提議する

[2] mean : 意地の悪い

[3] sinister : 陰険な

[4] camaraderie : 友愛，仲間意識

[5] even as : ～しているさなかにも

[7] the Ministry of Justice : 法務省
designate(d) : 指名する，任命する．野球の指名打者 (DH) は *designated hitter*.
civil liberties commissioners empowered . . . : いわゆる「子供の人権擁護員」.

[10] decides that *genkotsu* no longer belongs in Japanese schools : ゲンコツはもはや日本の学校にあってはならないと決める

[14] autocratic : 独裁的な
meek : おとなしい，屈従的な

[15] entails : requires; involves

[16] legislators : 法律制定者．要するに議員のこと．

[17] the system as is : 現状のままのシステム
assumption of the power of self-government inevitably comes with . . . : 自治の力を行使するとすれば，必然的に～を伴うことになる

[20] decision by consensus : 全体の同意による決定

[22] "good argument" : スポーツで両者が実力を発揮して好試合を戦うのが "good game" だとすれば，同じように議論で，両サイドがそれぞれの持ち味を出して，建設的に，かつ楽しく展開されるのが "good argument".

[23] taking charge : taking over; taking control

[25] oversee : 監督する

[27] congressperson : 連邦議会議員や州議会議員を意味する，男女共通語．

[28] a printed worksheet : いわゆる「プリント」.

SESSION 9

Behind *Front*: War Propaganda Photography and the 'Discovery of Text'

■

Ted Goossen

A FEW YEARS AGO, when I was about to start my first full-time teaching job at the advanced age of forty, I was told by the kindly Department Chair that one of my tasks would be to teach the non-western half of the 'World Religions' course. I protested that the only course I had ever taken on the subject had [5] been twenty years before; moreover, since it had been offered at eight-thirty in the morning, I had seldom attended class, and in the end had been forced to drop out. True, I had picked up a little information over the years from my studies in literature, but that was hardly enough to qualify me for what was being asked. 'But [10] don't you see,' the Chair said, the smile never leaving his face, 'that means that you don't have any of the old prejudices!'

The following article on the Japanese photographic propaganda magazine, *Front*, published between 1942 and 1945 for circulation to foreign countries, falls into much the same category. I [15] am not an expert on the art of photography and its history. Neither was I imprinted by the events and emotions engendered by World War Two. For example, when I have thought of 'imperialism' or 'militarism', it has usually been in terms of the United States, my country of origin, which I left in 1970 at the height of [20] the Vietnam War. This puts me in a very different situation than my parents' generation. For them, the words 'Japan' and 'milita-

テッド・グーセン氏はトロントのヨーク大学教授．日本文化に造詣が深く，目下オックスフォード大学出版局から出る日本の短篇小説アンソロジーを編纂中である．ここに載せた，戦時中の日本の海外向け宣伝写真をめぐる文章は，内容的には本格的な論文だが，文章はいたってしなやか．🅛

[3] the . . . Department Chair : 学科長．11 行目の the Chair も同じ．

[10] qualify me for : 私に〜の資格を与える

[14] *Front*, published between 1942 and 1945 . . . : 1989 年に平凡社から復刻版が出た．

[15] falls into much the same category : ほぼ同じ範疇に入る

[17] imprint(ed) : 強く印象づける，心に刻み込む
engendered by : 〜によって生まれた

rism' will be forever linked. Not long ago, for example, I gave a lecture on contemporary Japanese literature and culture to a large audience of senior citizens. When I finished, however, none of their questions dealt with the topics — the novels of Murakami Haruki and Yoshimoto Banana, the films of Itami Juzo, etc. — I [5] had discussed. Rather, they wanted to know my opinion on a separate issue: would Japan rearm to threaten the world once again?

To prepare to write this article, I had to 'discover' for myself what they were talking about. At the same time, I had to discover [10] what for me was a new genre. For *Front* is a prime example of a particular type of photography, used by state organizations for propaganda purposes. This genre was developed before and during the Second World War by a number of countries (*Front*, for example, was especially influenced by the Russian propaganda [15] magazine *Russia in Construction*, launched in 1930). Driven by the desire to win the 'propaganda war', and well aware of the potential power of the visual media, authorities poured vast amounts of resources into making *their* official photographic version of events the most compelling. This meant that at a time of great [20] scarcity, when it was almost impossible to obtain the materials necessary for their profession, photographers working in this genre were lavished with the best equipment that money could buy. In Japan's case, moreover, the priority given a project like *Front*, which was backed by the powerful General Staff Head- [25] quarters, protected its staff from any possible meddling by authorities — most particularly the Metropolitan Police Office and the Thought Control Police — who had every reason to be suspicious of the political views and lifestyles of what from the outside appeared to be a renegade group of thoroughly westernized [30] artists.

For my next 'discovery' as I moved through these new surroundings was the surprising makeup of the staff of *Front*. Never had I imagined that during the Pacific War, when liberal artists were forced into silence, thought conversion, or prison, there [35]

[7] rearm: 再軍備する

[11] genre: このフランス語の単語は，日本語では「ジャンル」だが，英語では「ジョーンラ」と聞こえる．

prime: chief; main

[12] state organizations: 国家組織

[17] potential power: 潜在力

[19] resources: 財源

[21] scarcity: 欠乏

[23] were lavished with: ～を惜しみなく与えられた

[24] priority: 優先権

[25] General Staff Headquarters: 参謀本部

[26] meddling: 干渉

[27] the Metropolitan Police Office: 警視庁

[28] the Thought Control Police: 憲兵隊

had every reason to: ～する理由がいくらでもあった

[30] renegade: 背教者の，裏切り者の

[33] makeup: 構成

[35] thought conversion: 思想の転向

could have been such a group of nonconformist, freethinking *individuals* allowed to live and work so freely. The founder of the *Tohosha* company that launched the project, Okada Sozo, for example, was a Shochiku movie actor whose light skin and 'exotic' good looks are credited to his mixed blood. (Interestingly, there are conflicting stories about his heritage: Yamaguchi Masao, for example, claims that Okada's mother was German, while Tagawa Sei'ichi, whose opinion seems to be more reliable, asserts that he had an English grandfather.) Urbane and debonair, Okada had lived in Germany and France, and had traveled extensively all across Europe, including Russia. Everything about him was anathema to the official view that to act 'foreign' was to be immoral and unpatriotic. Nor was Okada the only one who seemed 'un-Japanese'. The head of *Front*'s photographic section, Kimura Ihei, whose love affair with the Leica camera had helped make him Japan's best-known photographer, was thoroughly immersed in European contemporary culture, as was the magazine's art director, Hara Hiromu. A fourth man closely associated with this group, Nadori Yonosuke, would have probably been on the staff of *Front* too were it not for the fact that his pushy German wife had alienated some of the others (much as Ono Yoko would do with the Beatles some thirty years later). All in all, far from being right-wing propagandists, or even sympathizers to the militarists' cause, the people surrounding Japan's most famous war-time propaganda magazine were free-living and brightly-dressed bohemian types who included, so rumor had it, a number of committed Marxists.

Looked at from the perspective of the history of photography, this 'Marxist connection' is hardly surprising. For, as Kashiwagi Hiroshi and others have emphasized, it was from the revolutionary left — especially the Russian avant-garde, but also Italian futurism, Cubism, Dada, Surrealism, the Bauhaus, etc. — that the visual language of the war propaganda genre was borrowed 'virtually intact'. Moreover, these new modernist techniques — which included an emphasis on abstract form, the use of collage

[1] nonconformist： 社会の規範に従わない

[3] *Tohosha* . . .： 東方社

Okada Sôzô： 岡田桑三 (1903–83). 東方社，岡田については以下に詳述.

[5] are credited to： ～のせいだと言われている

[6] Yamaguchi Masao： 山口昌男 (1931–)，道化論をはじめ，驚異的に広範な研究活動を展開している文化人類学者.『FRONT』復刻版に，東方社の文化人コネクションを綴った「『フロント』をめぐる国際派知識人群像」を寄せている.

[7] Tagawa Sei'ichi： 多川精一 (1923–)，42 年原弘 (1903–86; 18 行目参照) の助手として東方社に入社. 45 年以降，装幀・レイアウトを専門に本作りに携わる.『FRONT』復刻版の監修者.

[8] . . . asserts that he had an English grandfather： 岡田桑三の息子一男も同様の証言をしている.

[9] Urbane and debonair： 都会的で人当たりのいい

[12] anathema： 何よりおぞましいもの

[14] Kimura Ihei, whose love affair with the Leica camera . . .： 木村伊兵衛 (1901–74)，スナップ写真の名手として，「ライカの木村」と言われた著名な写真家.

[16] was thoroughly immersed in： ～に浸りきっていた

[18] Hara Hiromu： 原弘. 原らをはじめとする「東方社コネクション」の戦後の動向について，山口昌男はつぎのように結ぶ.「その最良の部分が戦後，下中弥三郎の平凡社に結集した. 林達夫が編集長をつとめた『世界大百科事典』(全 32 巻) の装幀は原弘の手になるものであり (. . .) 原弘のデザインによる平凡社の刊行物に対する関わりは私が説くまでもなく人のよく知るところである.『太陽』のごときグラフィックな雑誌の刊行も原を抜きにしては語れない」

[19] Nadori Yonosuke： 名取洋之助 (1910–62)，33 年，木村，原らと「日本工房」を設立. 34 年，海外向け文化紹介雑誌『NIPPON』を刊行.

[20] pushy： 押しの強い

[21] alienate(d)： 遠ざける，仲を裂く

[24] the militarists' cause： 軍国主義思想

[26] so rumor had it： と噂されていたのだが

[27] committed Marxists： 熱心なマルクス主義者

[29] Kashiwagi Hiroshi： 柏木博 (1946–)，デザインに関する著書多数.

[31] Italian futurism： 1910 年代に発生. 機械文明を積極的に芸術に取り入れて，新しい美学を打ち立てようとしたが，比較的短命に終わった.

[32] the Bauhaus： 1919 年にドイツで設立された建築デザイン学校. その革新的モダニズム美学が及ぼした世界的影響は，デザインや建築の領域にとどまらない.

[33] 'virtually intact'： ここの部分，柏木博の原文は「ほとんどそのまま」.

and montage, and repetitive imagery — were augmented by the populist, commercial approach to photography being developed in the United States. Indeed, one of the formative influences on *Front* was a commercial ad campaign for the Japanese soap company *Kao Sekken* spearheaded by Kimura Ihei himself, while the [5] magazine he and others often used as a model was the glossy American publication *Life*! Unlike most other art forms, I was surprised to discover, 'ideological content' in photography was an easily exchangeable, almost irrelevant issue: the primary concern of the avant-garde photographers was to establish and forward [10] radically new visual styles which would rival those current in Europe. In short, the mission of *Front*'s founders, which they pursued with fiery zeal, was to develop what Susan Sontag later termed 'a grammar and, even more importantly, an ethics of seeing.' [15]

Taken together, these four preliminary 'discoveries' — the western perception of the 'Japanese menace', the genre called war propaganda photography, the extraordinary character of the 'authors' of *Front*, and the strangely disassociated relationship between photography and ideology then and now — suggest sev- [20] eral photographic metaphors. Viewed from one perspective, they could be taken to represent the four elements that go into the making of a picture: 'lens' (a western-made one in this case), 'backdrop', 'photographer', and 'style'. Alternatively, they could be seen as the four sides to the 'frame' surrounding my following [25] analysis of specific photographs. Like any frame, of course, they are defined as much by what they omit as by what they include — another critic with different background and training would inevitably produce yet another set of observations. Ultimately, I guess, any discovery of text is bound to be a personal [30] matter.

As my first such 'text', let me begin at the beginning, with the cover photo from the first issue of *Front*, the 'Navy Issue', which was published (in fifteen languages) in February, 1942. As you can see, it is a close-up shot of the profile of a young Japanese [35]

[1] montage: モンタージュ．複数の写真をつなぎあわせる写真術．いわゆる「モンタージュ写真」は identikit または composite という．
augmented: heightened

[2] populist, commercial approach: 大衆に訴えるような商業的アプローチ

[3] formative: 形成期の．*The child in her formative years.*

[9] exchangeable, almost irrelevant: 入れ替え可能な，ほとんど無関係な

[10] establish and forward radically: ～を打ち立て，ぐんぐん推し進める

[11] those current in Europe: ヨーロッパで実践されているスタイル

[12] mission: 使命
pursued with fiery zeal: 非常な情熱をもって追求した

[13] Susan Sontag: スーザン・ソンタグ．アメリカの批評家．*On Photography* という写真論がある(邦訳『写真論』晶文社)．ここの引用も，その冒頭から．

[16] preliminary: 前準備としての，予備的な

[17] menace: 脅威

[19] the strangely disassociated relationship: 不思議に分断された関係

[20] suggest: この動詞の主語は16行目からの these four preliminary 'discoveries' で，16～20行目のダッシュ内部は，その内容を具体的に要約している．

[21] photographic metaphors: 写真の発想を使った比喩

[24] backdrop: 背景
Alternatively: 別の見方をすれば．21行目の Viewed from one perspective を受けている．

[25] the four sides to the 'frame': これもまさに写真的な比喩．

[29] yet another: さらにもうひとつ別の

[35] profile: [próufail] 横顔

『FRONT』1-2号 1942(昭和17)年

sailor, shot from a low angle looking up. Above his head, just touching his cap, is the magazine's title (the word 'front', it should be noted, has several meanings — in this case, the dominant one is undoubtedly *zensen*, as in 'battlefront') . There are no objects in the background, only the sky, which is splashed diagonally with a band of cloud. The angle of the sailor's upper body, emphasized by the arrow-shaped insignia on his arm, is also arranged diagonally so that it powerfully intersects with the line in the sky in a kind of 'X' shape. The expression on the sailor's face is resolute, his gaze fixed on what lies ahead. We can tell by the way the light falls on his face that he is squinting into the sun. We imagine (although we have no way of knowing for sure) that he is standing on the deck of a large Navy vessel, searching the horizon for any sign of enemy submarines or planes.

I can assume from my reading in Japan's wartime ideology that this figure — so elemental in its 'man against the sky' pose that it is quite abstract, with no excess visual 'noise' to mar the image — is probably intended to convey a sense of purity and dynamism. Yet, what I notice through my 'western lens' is that, compared to the images of beautiful young men in uniform who grace the pages of the Nazi German propaganda magazine *Signal*, for example, this young man is not especially handsome. Had the photographer so desired, he could have found a more heroic-looking sailor (for we assume this is not a professional model) with fuller shoulders, smoother skin and a better haircut. His sailor's cap is not especially becoming, nor is his posture straight. Yet these 'flaws' add weight to the photograph, so that even though it is obviously posed, it comes across as a realistic image of a young warrior. Had his exterior been more beautiful, one imagines, the inner strength and determination of the sailor might not be so convincing.

With few exceptions, this 'normalcy' is the rule in Japanese war propaganda portraiture, setting it apart from examples of the genre produced by other nations. Japanese sailors, soldiers, and airmen, even when shot from a low camera angle in the typical

[2] the word 'front' . . . has several meanings : ここでは front に芸術の「最前線」という意味も読み込めそう．世間をごまかすための「隠れ蓑」という意味も front にはあるが，作る側はこの意味は意識していなかったであろう．

[3] dominant : most important

[5] splashed diagonally with a band of cloud : 帯状の雲が斜めに伸びている

[7] insignia : 記章

[8] intersect(s) : 交差する

[10] resolute : 確固とした，決然たる

[11] is squinting into the sun : 目を細くして太陽の方を見ている

[13] vessel : (大型の)船

[16] so elemental in its 'man against the sky' pose : 「空を背にした男」のポーズがきわめてストレートに押し出されているため

[17] excess : ここでは形容詞．「余分な」

[18] purity and dynamism : 純粋さと活力

[25] is not especially becoming : 特に似合ってもいない

[26] posture : 姿勢

[28] comes across as : ～として伝わってくる

[29] exterior : 外見

[32] 'normalcy' : 「普通らしさ」

[33] portraiture : 人物の撮り方

setting it apart from examples . . . : (そのため)他国の同様の例とは違ったものになっている

heroic pose, seldom project the larger-than-life aura of the Western hero. Moreover, such individual portraits are comparatively rare in the Japanese case. Instead, when the pages of *Front* include people at all (for the majority of the magazine's photographs are either of landscapes or of boats, planes, and other war machines) they tend to be arranged in small groups, or as masses of faceless troops. Individual valor, in short, is accorded less significance than teamwork, and the beauty of the human body, a common fetish in 'fascist aesthetics', is made to take second place to the grace and power of state-of-the-art armaments. Neither are the pages of *Front* graced with figures of recognizable national leaders like Stalin, Mussolini, or Hitler. Even when fashioning images for a foreign audience, it seems, the Japanese were reluctant to place too much emphasis on the image of the individual conquering hero.

This reluctance is particularly apparent when one turns to look at *Front*'s 'Air Force Issue', the fifth in the series, published in late 1943. Fighter pilots and their airplanes have been accorded the highest heroic status in the West since the First World War. This reflects what one can assume is a basic, unchanging reality. After all, alone above the clouds, with little to rely on but his individual skill, the fighter pilot is in fact far less dependent on his 'team' than his counterpart on the land or sea. Correspondingly, western war propaganda photography emphasizes the cult of the pilot, usually portrayed as an unhelmeted man standing beside his trusty plane, much like a cowboy beside his horse. Yet, *Front*'s Air Force issue has no photographs of this type. Instead, what we see most often are shots of soaring planes set against either banks of clouds or broad, foreign landscapes. Another frequent motif is that of 'life on the airfield': these photographs, when they show people at all, tend to show them in small groups, with native trainees being given special attention. Indeed, the most visible faces are not those of the Japanese pilots (which are usually partially hidden when they appear at all), but rather those of grateful Indian and Malay citizens who have presumably just been liber-

[1] project : 投げかける，伝える

the larger-than-life aura : 生身の人間よりも大きい感じがするオーラ．ベンヤミンの複製芸術論で論じられた「アウラの喪失」(写真などで芸術の複製が可能になって，「これひとつしかない」という魔力が消滅したこと）をはじめとして，かつては「アウラ」という表記が一般的だったが，最近は「オーラ」という表記も増えてきたようである．

[6] masses of faceless troops : 顔のない兵隊の群れ

[7] valor : 剛勇

accorded : given

[9] fetish : フェティシズムの対象．

take second place to : ～に次ぐ地位に甘んじる

[10] state-of-the-art armaments : 最新鋭の軍備

[11] grace(d) : 飾る

recognizable : 一目で誰だとわかる

[12] fashion(ing) : 作り上げる

[13] reluctant : ～したがらない

[19] This reflects what . . . unchanging reality : 「これは不変の根本的現実と考えられるものを反映している」．その「不変の根本的現実と考えられるもの」の内容は，以下に具体的に述べられている．

[21] but : except

[23] his counterpart on the land or sea : 陸軍・海軍で彼に(階級などで)相当する兵士

[24] the cult of the pilot : パイロット崇拝

[25] his trusty plane : trusty は「信頼のおける」．「愛用機」といったところ．

[28] soar(ing) : 空高く舞い上がる

[29] motif : モチーフ

[31] native trainees : 訓練を受けている現地の人間

[34] grateful : 感謝の表情を浮かべた

[35] who have presumably just been liberated : おそらくは解放されたばかり(という筋書き)の

ated by their Japanese saviors.

Yet, amidst all these reassuringly beautiful scenes, broken only occasionally by shots of falling bombs and diving fighters, there is one two-page montage two-thirds of the way through the issue that immediately caught my attention. Indeed, it would be no exaggeration to say that in this case the 'text' chose me, leading me to unexpected 'discoveries' about that darker side of Japan's war effort which *Front* was usually so careful to hide. In the process, I came to better understand the strong anti-Japanese emotions of my parents' generation, and the underlying causes of some of the 'Japan-bashing' that we see today.

Let us take a first look at those three photographs. On the left-hand page, we gaze up at the huge bulk (although it would be dwarfed by today's jets) of a Mitsubishi Zero, which, Americans were shocked to learn, was the most technologically advanced fighter plane involved in the Pacific War. The large photograph (one should note that *Front* was printed on glossy A3 paper) is centered on the nose of this powerful machine, which is so close at hand that we can easily imagine the deafening roar of its engine. Only half the monster is visible, although we can tell its overall shape from the line of three planes waiting in the distance, which are squeezed into the narrow triangle beneath its fuselage. The low camera angle, combined with the *closeness* of the close-up, instill an overpowering sense of unease in the viewer. This is hardly ameliorated by the half-hidden goggled face of the pilot peering down from the cockpit. With a mere pull on his stick, we realize uncomfortably, he can crush us under his wheels, or decapitate us with his propeller. Faced with this imposing mass of machine and its sinister faceless pilot, we can only feel vulnerable and totally insignificant. And if we escape, there are at least three more Zeros waiting for us!

Facing this image and occupying the greater part of the right-hand page is another close-up shot which, when viewed through a western lens at least, is even more unnerving. Perhaps a Japanese viewer would find nothing threatening in this photograph of

[2] amidst : 〜のただなかに
these reassuringly beautiful scenes : こうした，いかにも(安心して見ていられる)美しい情景

[3] diving fighters : 急降下する戦闘機

[4] two-page montage : 2ページにわたるモンタージュ．現物は本書の106〜107頁．
two-thirds of the way through the issue : 雑誌を3分の2くらい読み進んだあたりで

[6] 'text' : 「読み」の対象となるものなら，写真であれ映像であれバービー人形であれすべて「テクスト」である．

[8] In the process : そうするなかで

[13] the huge bulk : 巨体
it would be dwarfed by today's jets : 今日のジェット機と並べば，赤ん坊のようにしか見えないだろうが

[14] Zero : 零式戦闘機，零戦．

[17] glossy A3 paper : A3の光沢紙

[19] deafening roar : 耳をつんざくような轟音

[21] overall shape : 全体の形

[22] fuselage : 胴体

[24] instill : しみ込ませる

[25] ameliorated : softened
goggled : 戦闘用のゴーグルをつけた

[26] With a mere pull on his stick : 操縦桿をぐいと引きさえすれば

[27] decapitate : 〜の首を切る

[28] imposing mass : 堂々たる巨体

[29] sinister : 不気味な，邪悪そうな
vulnerable : 無防備な

[34] is even more unnerving : さらにいっそう不気味である

a man wearing a kendo mask, holding his practice wooden sword at his side. To one unfamiliar with perhaps the weirdest of Japan's traditional martial arts, however, the strange garb speaks of dark and ancient mysteries. Again, we are uncomfortably close, and looking from chest level, so that his eyes seem to be [5] staring over our heads. And what inhuman eyes they are! There is no emotion in their gaze, no hint of human compassion. Encased in its steel grid, criss-crossed in shadow, the face that looks out from behind the mask cannot be 'read' for any meaning — it is cold and enigmatic, and seems to be awaiting orders like some [10] programmed robot.

The structural similarities between these two photographs — the use of extreme close-ups, the massive, abstract shapes in center-frame set against an empty sky, the low camera view, the blurring of the lines dividing man and machine — reinforce, through [15] their repetition, a sense of claustrophobic fear in the foreign viewer. Ironically, here all the basic elements of the 'modernist style', born in revolution and developed in commercialism, are marshaled to their fullest effect to convey the dark threat of Japanese militarism! [20]

Indeed, it is almost with a sigh of relief that one turns to the smaller photograph at the bottom of the right-hand page, which looks down on the rather chaotic scene of about fifty men engaged in kendo practice. Finally, it seems, one has room to breathe. Yet, on closer inspection, this photograph is hardly reas- [25] suring to the foreign viewer either, for there is no discernible order to the exercise, and still no faces to the soldiers, most of whose backs are turned away from the camera. In fact, there is something most unsettling about the way this least dramatic of the three photos fits with the others in a seamless whole. [30]

I must admit, I was a bit taken aback to be moved so strongly by these two pages. It goes without saying that I had seen many other images of 'Japan at war' before: in books, movies, and even the comic books of my youth, I had encountered the full range of brutal Japanese soldiers, prison guards, and suicide attacks. [35]

[1] his practice wooden sword : 練習用の竹刀

[2] perhaps the weirdest of Japan's traditional martial arts : 「日本の伝統的武道のなかでもっとも異様なもの」．たしかに，柔道，空手に較べて剣道の世界的浸透度はいまひとつ(むろん，フェンシングも非西洋人の目には十分異様だが)．

[3] garb : 衣装

[5] chest level : 胸の高さ

[7] no hint of human compassion : 人間らしい情のかけらも感じられない
Encased in its steel grid, criss-crossed in shadow : 鋼鉄の格子に収まり，十字模様の影に包まれて

[10] enigmatic : 謎めいた

[14] the blurring of the lines : 境界線をぼやけさせること

[15] reinforce : 「強化する」．主語は 12 行目の The structural similarities between these two photographs. ダッシュのなかはその具体的説明．

[16] claustrophobic fear : 密室に閉じ込められたような(息苦しい)恐怖感

[19] marshal(ed) : 並べる，整列させる

[23] chaotic : 混沌とした

[24] one has room to breathe : やっと一息つける

[26] there is no discernible order : 見たところ何の秩序も見当たらない

[29] unsettling : 不気味な．前ページ 34 行の unnerving に近い．

[30] fits with the others in a seamless whole : ほかの写真と合わさって，継ぎ目のない一個の全体を形成している

[31] was a bit taken aback : いささかうろたえた

[35] suicide attacks : 特攻隊員による自爆攻撃

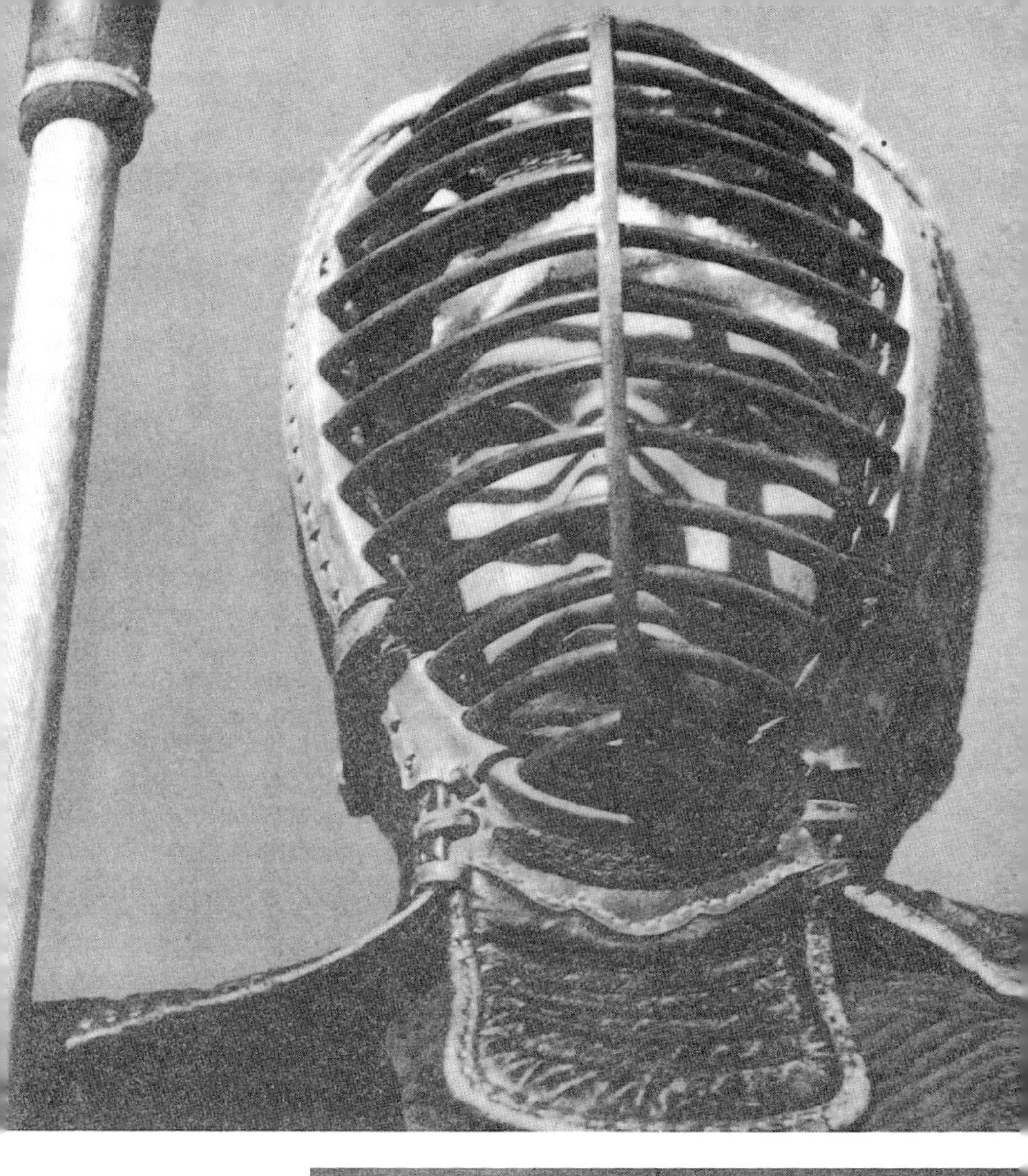

HE EMBODIMENT F TRADITION AND SCIENCE

None, however, had had a similar impact. Why? One reason, I
suppose, is the power of the visual images *as images*, a testimony
to the technical mastery of their creators. Another possible cause,
however, is suggested by John Dower in his book, *War Without
Mercy*. There, Dower notes that the fear of the Orient has three [5]
main strands: '. . . Asian mastery of Western knowledge and
technique; access to mysterious powers and "obscure and dreadful things"; and mobilization of the yellow horde . . . . Whether
led by China or Japan, this was the essence of the Yellow Peril.'

It is striking that each of the three photos in our text can be [10]
connected to one of these three 'strands'. Certainly, the Zero
fighter, with its massive power and deafening noise, is a perfect
evocation of the frightening side of the 'Asian mastery of Western
knowledge and technique'. Just as clearly, the portrait of the
kendo warrior, with his strange garb, phallic staff, and shadowy [15]
expressionless face, speaks to the foreign viewer of 'mystery, obscure and dreadful'. Finally (although perhaps least obviously)
the confusing, faceless swarm of soldiers engaged in kendo practice does call up the image of the 'yellow horde' with all its insect-
like connotations. I had always considered myself immune to the [20]
Yellow Peril Syndrome, which I connected with racism, igno-
rance, and the legacy of the War. Perhaps, however (and this
could be seen as my final 'discovery'), given the right set of
stimuli, I am not as far removed from it as I thought.

Perhaps, too, I was affected by the caption wedged in between [25]
the three photographs: 'The Embodiment of Tradition and Science'. In one sense, of course, this caption is quite unnecessary: as
we have seen, the montage of images speaks for itself, making
further comment extraneous. Yet, as one version of a phrase that
has appeared over and over again in a variety of forms since the [30]
old days of *Wakon Yosai* ('Japanese Spirit, Western Technology')
— and which could be traced back even further to the *Wakon
Kansai* ('Japanese Spirit, Chinese Technology') era — these catch-
words have the effect of extending the significance of our 'text'
back into the distant past, and up to the present day. [35]

[2] testimony: 証明，あかし

[6] Asian mastery of . . . : アジア人が〜をマスターしたこと

[7] obscure and dreadful things: 知られざる恐ろしいもの

[8] mobilization of the yellow horde: 文字どおり訳せば「黄色い群れの動員」.

[9] the Yellow Peril: 黄禍，という訳語は幸い死語になった．西洋が，東洋の進出・勢力拡張に対して抱く危機感を表わした言葉.

[11] strands: strand は本来，ロープなどを構成する 1 本 1 本の細い糸のこと．そこから一般化して，「構成要素」.

[12] is a perfect evocation of . . . : 〜を完璧に喚起する

[15] phallic staff: 男根のような竿

[18] swarm: 群れ

[19] with all its insect-like connotations: 「昆虫のようなイメージがこびりついた」. connotations は「言外の意味」.

[20] immune to: 〜に免疫がある

[21] racism: 人種偏見

[22] legacy: 遺産

[23] given the right set of stimuli: しかるべき刺激を与えられさえすれば

[24] not as far removed from it as I thought: 「思っていたほど東洋の偏見から自由ではない」.

[25] the caption wedged in between the three photographs: 3 枚の写真のあいだに押し込まれた表題

[26] Embodiment: 体現

[28] speaks for itself: （表題の必要もないほど）雄弁に物語っている

[29] extraneous: unnecessary

For it seems that the ways in which Japan advertises itself have not changed all that much. Today's commercial propagandists, some working for the same companies that backed *Front* (Mitsui, Mitsubishi, and Sumitomo), still publicize the glories of Japan's 'unique union of tradition and technology' through glossy [5] graphic designs, not for the purposes of intimidation, but in order to sell us more computers and automobiles. We, in turn, respond to these visual images with our own stereotyped pictures of faceless robotic *sarariman*, and insect-like Asian hordes.

Finally, I believe the main reason I was so taken aback by these [10] stereotyped pictures encapsulating the dark side of the Japanese myth was that they were produced, not by 'prejudiced' Westerners, but by Japanese of the most cosmopolitan sort. Given their skill and international background, we might expect that they were aware of the reaction the images would elicit. If so, what [15] was their intent? To intimidate their foreign audience at a time of increasing desperation (for by 1943 the tide of battle had already turned against Japan)? To reveal, in a rare display of honesty (for *Front*, like all war propaganda magazines, as a rule aestheticized and sanitized the national war effort), the hidden truth about the [20] militarists' cause? Or were they actually *unaware* of the manner in which the kendo warrior, for example, would likely be viewed by their foreign audience? For me, this issue of authorial intent, so basic yet so difficult to ascertain, seems to have eluded my grasp. Please forgive me, then, if I leave it to you, dear readers, to make [25] this final 'discovery' on your own!

[1] have not changed all that much：「それほど変わっちゃいない」．論文調のなかに紛れ込む口語体が効果的．

[6] intimidation： 威嚇

[11] encapsulating：「～を凝縮した形で表わしている」．encapsulate の文字どおりの意味は「カプセル (capsule) に入れる」．

[13] Given . . .： ～を考えるなら

[15] elicit： 引き出す，生み出す

[16] at a time of increasing desperation： 戦況が次第に絶望的になってきた時期に

[18] in a rare display of honesty：（ふだんの仮面をかなぐり捨てて）珍しく本心をさらけ出して

[19] aestheticized and sanitized： 美的に，毒を抜いて仕立てた

[23] issue of authorial intent： 作者がどういう意図をもっていたかという問題

[24] seems to have eluded my grasp： 私には捉えきれなかったようだ

『FRONT』はどのくらい「役に立った」のか．

■

「. . .『FRONT』は，グラフィックデザインの技術や製版・印刷の面で，戦前の出版物の水準をはるかに超えるものであった．厳しい戦時下で，当時の最高の技術を結集して製作された他に類例のない印刷物であった．しかし，その本来の目的である宣伝物としての効果はどうであったかということになると，これはもう，何もわかっていないのである．

（. . .）あの膨大な量の『FRONT』がどこに運ばれ，どういう人に配られたのかほとんどわかっていないのである．『FRONT』は軍の諸機関が買い上げる形で東方社の手を離れた．戦闘行動に明け暮れていた軍の機関に，こうした悠長な宣伝物を計画的に配布する余裕などなかったことは十分考えられるし，ましてその効果測定などまったく念頭になかったであろう．

印刷物として，50年後の今日見ても驚くような出来栄えでありながら，宣伝物という本来の目的から判断すると，その効果はほとんどゼロに近かったとしか思われないのである．そうしたことを知りながら当時の幹部スタッフは，『FRONT』を作り続けることによって戦争の嵐の過ぎるのを待っていたのではなかろうか」（多川精一「『FRONT』，その製作現場」）．

SESSION 10

Something I Encountered in Japan and How It Followed Me Home

■

Dan McLeod

I GOT USED TO unexpected little things happening pretty regularly during my first stay in Japan a little over thirty years ago. Most of them were pleasant surprises like the smell of *katori senko* on summer nights in Maebashi or the satisfying chewiness of dried squid during long movies I only half understood. But a [5] couple were shockers. The first was hearing from a stranger on the Maebashi-Kiryu train that President Kennedy had been assassinated. The grim implications of this event and the second, my introduction to Japan's college admission examinations, haunt me to this day. I never gave my country's mindless gun violence a [10] thought before Kennedy was shot, but over the years it's become an unavoidable, in-your-face daily event on the news. And that business of entrance exams which at the time seemed just another curiosity of Japanese culture appears to have trailed in the wake of the ship that carried me back to the United States. From the [15] sixties my country has been accelerating the development of its own variations on this grueling rite of passage.

Because I was an undergraduate in the fifties, I didn't have to take an entrance exam for admission to a rather selective university (U.C. Berkeley) and a semester later to an even more selective [20] liberal arts college (Pomona). All it took was decent grades in high school, a couple of letters from teachers vouching for my

1994年ニューヨーク大学で大規模な「ビート文学」の大会(というかビート仲間の最初の出会いの50年祭)があって，ダン・マクラウドとぼくとは，寮の同じ部屋に泊まることになった．夜になると，ダンはいつも安物のジンかウォッカを取り出して，ストレートで飲み出す．いつもたくさん仕事を抱えて，でも仕事は遅くて(異様にこだわる)，いつもズリズリの格好をしていて，見た感じはなんともチャランポラン．でも人情家で，日本からの留学生が事故に遭えば，父親のように病院に通い詰める．最後のところは真似できないが，ぼく自身の生活と似ている気もする．サン・ディエゴ州立大学，サン・マルコス州立大学教授を歴任．アメリカの統一学力試験の委員にも長く関わっていたので，入学試験の問題を扱ってもらうことにした．㋚

[2] a little over thirty years ago：ケネディ暗殺は1963年．その年ぼくは同じ群馬の中学校に入学，英語の勉強をはじめたことになる．

[4] the satisfying chewiness of dried squid：この表現からすると Dan が食べたと記憶しているのは「するめ」だろうか．この5年前までぼくは前橋に住んでいたのだが，映画館で「のしいか」を買ってもらって食べた記憶はたしかにある．

[7] Maebashi-Kiryu train：国鉄両毛線の電車は，正確には Takasaki-Kiryu（または Takasaki-Oyama）train と書くべきであるが，この誤記は「前橋人」の意識を正しく伝えている．

[9] haunt：霊のようにとりつく

[12] in-your-face daily event：毎日顔をつきあわせる出来事

[13] just another curiosity：数々の奇妙なことがらのうちのひとつ

[17] grueling：人をへとへとにさせる(ほど消耗な)
rite of passage：通過儀礼(社会で一人前として認められるための試練)

[18] an undergraduate：(a graduate student に対して)学部生

[20] U.C. Berkeley：U.C. は University of California.「バークレー」と聞いて，60年代学園紛争の口火を切った大学というイメージをもつ人は少なくなった(今この大学はビジネス教育の充実で知られている)．ダンが行っていたのは50年代のことだから，キャンパスの雰囲気もずいぶん整然としていただろう．1967年ころの映像なら映画『卒業』で手軽に見ることができる．Sather Gate を出ると Telegraph Avenue が南へ伸びて，そこはかつて学生と警官隊との衝突も繰り返されたが，今は60年代ヒッピー系のファッションを売る屋台が並ぶばかり．

[21] Pomona：カリフォルニア州クレアモントの Pomona College は創立1887年．liberal arts college (→ 123ページの注 [13] 参照)としては，ミシシッピー以西で最高といわれる．ちなみに，留学生受け入れの基準になる TOEFL scores の最低点は600点．

academic promise, and the writing of a short personal essay testifying to the sincerity of my desire to study at those schools. When I decided to go on to graduate school I was encouraged to take something called the GRE (Graduate Record Examination), but it wasn't absolutely required in the late fifties. I was admitted on the basis of my undergraduate record, a few more letters from indulgent teachers, and another earnest personal essay. So, I was surprised a couple of years later when, as a graduate student on a Fulbright Fellowship, I confronted my first admission examination in Japan.

It should have been easy. A Japanese friend showed me a copy of the English language section of Tokyo University's entrance examination that had been printed in *Asahi Shinbun*. He wanted to know what I thought of it, so I picked up a pencil and had a go at it. As a doctoral candidate in English, I didn't feel much challenged by a multiple choice test designed to measure a Japanese high school student's command of my native language, but it was harder for me to deal with than I had anticipated. The problem was that a good many of the items offered possible answers that looked equally correct to me. It is, after all, possible to say the same thing in as many different ways in English as it is in any other language. Still, my friend assured me, there was only one correct answer for each of the items I was puzzling over. In the end I had to guess at a lot of them, and after checking my responses with the answer key that *Asahi* had thoughtfully provided, my friend's assessment of my performance was that it might not have been up to *Todai* standards.

Until that humbling experience I hadn't understood how my own national university students could have studied English for six or more years and not be able to join in on the simple conversation practices I had developed from their text. The readings in the text, mostly literary selections, were rather challenging, and the grammatical notes on the lower half of each page were complex and extensive. Because the only English in these notes were examples, I wasn't always sure what they explained. Beyond the

[4] GRE： 大学院受験のための，適性および専門学力試験．

[7] indulgent teachers： i.e. teachers who, when they write letters of reference, tend to be too sweet to their students.
personal essay： アメリカの主要大学院では，志望動機，研究課題，将来の抱負などを，かなり詳しく書かせてくれる．

[9] Fulbright Fellowship： 米国と他国との留学・教授招聘プログラムの中で文系関係者にとってこれが一番門は広い．ダンは今までに4回もフルブライトの世話になっていて，「これはギネス・レコードもんだ」と強調する．

[12] Tokyo University： 実際こうも言われるけど，正式な英語名称は the University of Tokyo.

[14] had a go at it： とりかかった

[15] didn't feel much challenged： i.e. thought that the questions would be very easy.

[25] responses： 「答えを出した」というよりは「応えたにすぎない」という語感．

[28] humbling： 屈辱的．25行目の thoughtfully と同様，ユーモラスな皮肉．
my own national university： 群馬大学のこと．

Think You Understand English?
Here are some sample questions from an English test that is part of the entrance exam at W. University in Tokyo.

1. Choose the one word that does not belong.
A. Calmly. **B.** Friendly. **C.** Patiently.
D. Quickly. **E.** Sweetly.
Answer: B.
Reason: A, C, D, and E, all derive from adjectives while the word friendly *doesn't.*

2. Supply a word in the parentheses so that each pair of sentenses have the same meaning.
I. (略)
II. **A.** This is really a very challenging job.
B. This is a very difficult job but ( ) doing.
III. **A.** You should have made sure I was expecting you before you came to see me.
B. You should have ( ) your appointment before you came to see me.
Answers: II. *worth;* III. *confirmed; No other answers are correct.*

日本の入試問題は，ダンを困らせた30年前から変わったろうか．「ニューヨーク・タイムズ」(1995年8月4日) の日本の英語教育に関する記事に，こんな問題の例が紹介されていた．1.は D. ではいけないのだろうか．ほかは「態度」を表わす言葉(それもみな「やさしさ」「穏やかさ」に関係する)で，Quickly だけ「動作」に関わるわけだし．2.の II. は考え込んでしまう．a very difficult job というだけで challenging の内容はほぼ言い切れているし，傍目には not worth doing なことでも，本人の「気持ちを駆り立てる」仕事というのはあるし．．．． III. の別解：checked, double-checked, reconfirmed 等．your appointment が目的語としてなければ，You should have called me . . . ですむんですけどね．

readings and grammatical analyses the text provided no material for actually practicing the language, so I generated some exercises from the readings and spent a lot of class time in a mostly futile effort to involve my students in them.

Since language is basically sound, listening and speaking [5] seemed worth practicing. And besides that was how I'd been trained to teach it the summer before at the University of Michigan's English Language Institute. The readings in the Michigan texts were entirely conversational dialogues. What I hadn't realized before my friend introduced me to the Japanese [10] entrance examination was that my students had not been studying English in the ordinary way for six years, but for examinations like the one I might not have passed. My students read their selections silently (probably translating them just as silently into Japanese as they went), and were prepared to discuss [15] them in Japanese although they would have preferred to simply listen to one of their other teachers explain it to them — in Japanese, of course. That's what the entrance examinations had done to language study in the sixties, and I suspected they had a similar impact on other subjects. [20]

A year or so later, my doctorate completed and with a pleasant job in my hometown's oldest and largest university, I became aware that the U.S. was rapidly developing an admissions testing program. This awareness came in the form of an invitation to read college "placement" tests for Educational Testing Service, a com- [25] pany that had been around less than twenty years but already so well known in educational circles that it was usually referred to as ETS. It was best known for its "aptitude" tests. The Scholastic Aptitude Test (SAT), Graduate Record Examination, Graduate Management Aptitude Test (GMAT), and Law School Aptitude [30] Test (LSAT) were being used as a part of the admissions process for undergraduate, graduate and professional schools all over the country. ETS also had begun a program of "achievement" tests called Advanced Placement which, if passed, gave high school

[2] I generated . . . : それだけでなく，ダンは英語の音声教材の作成にも精を出した．昭和 38 年，テープといえばオープン・リールのころである．

[4] futile : [fjúːtl / fjúːtail] having no useful result

[12] studying English in the ordinary way : 西洋文化摂取の初期の時代，大学は高給料で外国人教師を雇い，授業は半分近くが英語等で行なわれるという状況で，その当時の学生は，けっこう英米人と対等にやりあえる英語力を身につけた．だが英語教育の普及にともない，その「国風化」が進んで，「英語で」教える「正則英語」に対し日本人が英語を読み解く術を指南する「変則英語」がカリキュラムに入っていった．その「変則英語」が「変則」の意識をもたぬまま「英語」として学校教育に居すわってから，すでに 4 世代めに入っている．

for six years : 6 年間「読み」ならやってきたか，というと，これが怪しい．文部省検定教科書を 6 年ぶん足した英文の分量は，ふつうの英語のペーパーバック何ページ分にあたるかというと，これがほんの数十ページなのです．

[19] in the sixties : 現在でも状況は基本的にそう大きくは動いていないようですけどね．まず大学教師が受験問題を改善していきながら，こういう勉強をしていかないとダメだよと，世の中にアピールしていくことが必要なんですね．

[21] doctorate : 大学で最初は生物を学んだというダンの学位は英文学の博士号．

[24] invitation to read college "placement" tests : つまり，採点委員を委託されたということ．"placement" test の説明は次ページの本文に出ています．

[26] around : present; existing. "*Is Alice around today*?" : きょう来てる？

[29] SAT : 発音は「エス・エイ・ティー」

[30] Law School : 4 年制大学を出たあとで入る法律家養成機関．

students credit for college level courses that could be transferred to almost any college or university. Those students who passed a number of Advanced Placement tests in high school also increased their chances of being admitted to highly selective schools. The Test of English as a Foreign Language (TOEFL), required of immigrant and international students, is an ETS test used to measure achievement as well as for admissions and placement. Put together, "placement" tests, (which place admitted students in appropriate math, language and writing courses), "aptitude" tests (which attempted to predict college performance), and "achievement" tests (which aimed to measure specific subject mastery), were collectively serving the same function as admission tests in Japan — identification of an educational elite for a social system based on merit and driven by money and access to high status jobs.

Just as Japan preceded the U.S. in the serious institutionalizing of admissions tests, so China's use of qualifying tests to sort out an elite from ordinary citizens predates their appearance in western civilizations — by more than a thousand years. Chinese historians have traced the use of civil service admissions tests as far back as the Chou Dynasty (1122–256 B.C.E.), and by the Sung Dynasty (960–1279) the examination process was clearly the path to wealth and social status in China since, unlike western civilizations, the power of hereditary aristocrats had pretty much disappeared by then. They had been replaced by the government bureaucracies, and appointments to them depended on examination performance more than any kind of family influence.

For the socially ambitious, studying for these examinations became a way of life that frequently extended into middle age. Successful examination performance required virtual memorization of the Confucian classics and their most important commentaries as well as certain other gentlemanly accomplishments (women, of course, were excluded) such as the ability to compose poetry and essays that reflected and expressed Confucian values. While performing these tasks under strict testing conditions was

[1] credit for college level courses that could be transferred . . . : つまり大学に入る前に，その大学の単位をあらかじめ取っておくということができるわけ．

[12] collectively serving the same function as admission tests in Japan : 「全体としてみると日本の入試と同じ機能を果たしている」．とはいえ，考査の名前のつけ方ひとつをとってみても，日米の教育についての文化的ちがいは歴然としている．それぞれの生徒のプライドを大切にすることを初等・中等教育の理想とするアメリカでは，成績のよさ，悪さによって当落を決めることに一般的な抵抗感があり，そのためにAptitude（適性），Placement（配置）というような婉曲的言い方がされるわけだが，社会での競争原理が「受験」という形で十代に集中的にかかってくるような社会では，「学力選抜試験」という，ハードな言い方が好まれるのだろう．

[16] serious : 本格的な

[17] qualifying tests : 資格試験．*You're not qualified for the position.*

[21] Chou [dʒou] Dynasty : 周王朝

B.C.E. : B.C. のあとに E がつく形はあまりお目にかからないけれど，これは "Before the Christian Era" または "Before the Common Era" の略．

Sung [suŋ] Dynasty : 宋王朝

[24] hereditary aristocrats : （家柄によって要職につく）世襲貴族

pretty much : かなりの部分．（現在のアメリカでは文章に出てきてもとくに「くだけた」印象は与えない．）

[26] appointments to them : 官僚組織への登用

[28] the socially ambitious : 立身出世主義者．ダンは Beat Generation（19 ページ）に属する一人として，こうした生き方への軽蔑をガソリンにして若い時代を生きてきた．この文章は中立公平な立場から書いているわけだけれど，22～23 行目 "the path to wealth and social status" などの表現にどうしても「地」が出てくる——ように思えるのはぼく自身の偏向かな？

[31] Confucian classics : 「論語」をはじめとする儒学の古典．Confucius : 孔子．

an impressive accomplishment, it did not necessarily demonstrate those qualities required of government officials.

The problems attendant on this classical Chinese system of social selection have lessons for us today. Once China became subject to the intrusions of foreign powers and western ideas, it became painfully apparent that the narrow literary and historical education of its leaders, an education determined by examinations that assessed the same skills and content they had during the Sung Dynasty, was insufficient preparation for dealing with the large scale social changes that were transpiring from the eighteenth century. Still, the examination system persisted with little change until 1905 when it was formally abolished by the empress dowager. But by that time the Chinese empire was in a shambles.

Examination fervor in Japan dates back to my first stay in the early sixties, and like the "economic miracle" that was taking off about the same time, I hardly noticed. *Ronin* life for those students who'd failed to win a place in a university of their choice was not as common as it was soon to be, nor had the *juku* and *yobiko* industry become big time. Perhaps its most obvious manifestation back then was the growing uniformity and inflexibility of the high school curriculum as it focused ever more intently on entrance examination preparation after a decade or so of American influenced innovations. And except for those schools attached to universities where students were almost assured of admission, extracurricular activity was decreasing. Back in the U.S., I was used to hearing older people complain about the idleness of the younger generation and how high school standards had declined, but in Japan people were beginning to talk about the decline of adolescent life in the face of ever keener competition for places in prestigious universities. The number of Japanese universities had more than tripled since the war, but admission to these newer universities did not confer the same social advantages that admission to the former imperial universities or a few of the oldest private universities still did.

In the U.S. the pressure for admission to highly selective

[5] powers : 列強

[6] painfully apparent : 日本語でも「痛いほどよくわかる」とか「痛感する」というが, "painfully aware" などの言い方も英語の頻出パターン.

[10] transpiring : becoming visible; occurring gradually

[12] the empress dowager : 皇太后. 半世紀以上にわたって清朝の最高実力者として君臨した西太后のこと.

[13] in a shambles : in complete disorder. "shambles" はつねに単数形扱い.

[14] Examination fervor : 過熱した受験競争

in the early sixties : 大学受験者の激増により「浪人」「狭き門」という言い方がジャーナリズムを賑わわせるようになったのは, たしかに 60 年代前半のこと.

[18] not as common as it was soon to be : まもなくありふれた光景になるのだが, 当時はそれほどでもなかった.

[19] become big time : 一大産業になる

manifestation : あらわれ.

[22] after a decade or so . . . : アメリカに影響された改革が 10 年あまり進められたにもかかわらず, というニュアンスがある.

schools has never been as intense as it is in Japan because the connection between American universities and the kind of careers open to their graduates has never been as close as it has been in Japan since the *Meiji* era. Furthermore, lifetime employment with a government agency or a single company has never been as common in the U.S. where careers are usually advanced by changing employers or becoming an entrepreneur. The prestige of the universities American students graduate from might have some influence on their first jobs, but after that they're on their own. So why, you might ask, has the entrance examination enterprise grown so impressively here over the last forty years? [5] [10]

Among the most selective American schools are the four national military academies, a dozen or so small liberal arts colleges, and the Ivy League universities — especially Harvard, Yale, Princeton and a few others in New England and Stanford on the West coast. Most of these schools have been around for over a hundred years, and excepting the military academies, are all private. While the military academies accept only eleven to fourteen percent of their applicants, the others (even Harvard, Yale, and Princeton) usually accept about twenty to twenty-five percent of those who apply. Since very few who apply to these highly selective schools are unqualified, something more than terrific high school grades, impassioned letters of recommendation, and an impressive record of extracurricular talents and activities (music, athletics, volunteer social work and the like) is required to distinguish the most qualified applicants. And so we add admissions tests. [15] [20] [25]

Still, the social pressure to gain admission to even the most selective American universities is probably less than it is for even moderately prestigious universities in Japan. And if applicants fail to gain admission to a selective school the first time they try, there is no need for American students to waste a year or more of their lives in *yobiko*. Instead, they can enroll in a less selective four year school or even a two year junior college, and transfer to a more selective school on the basis of the grades they've earned [30] [35]

[7] entrepreneur： [ɑ:ntrəprənə́:r] 訳語としては最近日本語に定着してきた「起業家」がぴたり．独立独歩の「開拓者」に価値を置くアメリカで，昔気質の人間は，他人に雇われる生き方を敬遠する傾向が強い．

[13] military academies： ニューヨーク州ウェスト・ポイントの陸軍士官学校(U.S. Military Academy)が創立1802年で最古．その他，海軍および海兵隊の士官学校(U.S. Naval Academy)がメリーランド州アナポリスに，空軍士官学校(U.S. Air Force Academy)がコロラド州コロラド・スプリングズに，沿岸警備隊の士官学校(U.S. Coast Guard Academy)がコネチカットのニュー・ロンドンにある．すべて5年制．

liberal arts colleges： 独自のカラーをもつ少数精鋭型の大学．文学・政治・経済・歴史・芸術・心理・生命科学等の「教養」諸科目を学ぶ学生が数の上では多く，law school, business school, medical school 等の大学院を持つものも少なくない．マサチューセッツの Amherst, Williams, Wellesley, ペンシルヴァニアの Swarthmore, コネチカット Wesleyan 等の有名校を筆頭に全米で160大学ほどがこのカテゴリーに入る．

[15] a few others： Ivy League を構成するのは，ダンの挙げた3校の他に，ニューヨーク市の Columbia, ロード・アイランドの Brown, ペンシルヴァニアの Pennsylvania, ニューヨーク州山間部の Cornell, それにマサチューセッツの Dartmouth. それ以外の「名門」および「難関」ユニヴァーシティとしては，ワシントン＝ボルチモア地区の Johns Hopkins, Georgetown, 南部の Duke, Vanderbilt, Virginia, テキサスの Rice, シカゴの Chicago Univ. と North Western, カトリック系の Notre Dame, 工科大学の MIT（マサチューセッツ）と Cal Tech（カリフォルニア）等々が有名．

[30] moderately prestigious： そこそこに箔のある

[33] enroll in . . . even a two year junior college, and transfer . . .： Pall Alkebulan が息子の Bomani に期待しているのはまさにこのコース(→ 32ページ)．

there without bothering to retake an entrance examination. Unlike students in Japanese universities, a significant proportion of American students, particularly those in large state universities, either drop or flunk out during their first year or two of school — thus opening places for these transfers. My university is part of [5] the State University of California, the largest system of universities in the world, and entering juniors outnumber entering freshman.

Just as most Americans will work for many different companies or government agencies in the course of their careers, so most [10] American college graduates will have attended more than one college or university before they graduate. And since undergraduate admissions are handled by university admissions offices rather than by academic departments as in Japan, it is not at all unusual for students to change their major department, some- [15] times a number of times, before they take their degrees. But even in this fluid atmosphere of relatively easy admissions, transfers and changes of majors, the role played by entrance examinations on the American academic scene has increased in almost every year since I returned from Japan, and the one that's experienced [20] the most rapid growth since the sixties, and generated the most controversy as well, is the Scholastic Aptitude Test (SAT) which nearly two million high school juniors and seniors take every year.

In the U.S. higher education is overwhelmingly public and ac- [25] cessible to nearly everyone. Of the more than three thousand fully accredited American colleges and universities only about two hundred can be described as at all selective, and most of these accept at least half the students who apply for admission. A third of our universities accept 90% of their applicants and more than [30] half accept 80%. Of the selective private colleges and universities, only about forty reject as many as half their applicants, and only six reject as many as 80%. Very few American high school students find it difficult gaining admission to a good university; their problem is financing higher education (a major reason for [35]

[1] without bothering to :　わざわざ〜したりせず

[4] either drop or flunk out :　dorp out することと flunk out することの違いについては，35 行目以降に説明がある．

[5] My university :　ジェリー・グリズウォルドやラリー・マキャフリーの(年長の)同僚として San Diego State University で長年教えてから，ダンは数年前，アメリカで 20 年ぶりに新設された公立大学の California State University at San Marcos に移った．

[6] the State University of California :　カリフォルニアには，University of California 系列に属する，より prestigious な州立大学システムがあって，State University 系の大学は，それとは別のシステムとして運営されている．

[7] juniors :　(大学) 3 年生．

[14] academic departments :　(教授たちで構成する)学部や学科

[17] fluid :　流動的な

[23] juniors and seniors :　senior は高校の最上級学年(4 年または 3 年)，junior はその 1 年下．

[25] overwhelmingly public :　「名門」はほとんどが私立だが，全体の学生数をみると州立大学が圧倒している．部分的に州政府からの金でまかなわれている州立大学は，University of California 等を例外として，州内からの受験者はかなり容易に入学できる．

[26] fully accredited :　正規の大学として認可を得た．

[35] financing higher education . . . and maintaining course grades :　学資を稼ぎながら大学に通い，しかもきちんと単位をとっていく．

dropping out) and maintaining course grades (which leads to
flunking out). Why then do more than fifteen hundred colleges
and universities bother to require applicants to take the SAT?

The reason an aptitude test such as the SAT, rather than one
that measures academic achievement, is the most widely ac- [5]
cepted admissions examination in the U.S. might sound strange
in Japan where achievement tests alone determine who will and
will not be admitted. Most universities use the SAT not so much
to select the most qualified students, but to identify those students who will not flunk out during their freshman year. Many [10]
fine public universities lose as many as half the freshmen they
admit, most of them during their first year — a situation unimaginable in Japan. And neither American or Japanese universities
can afford to lose the students they've accepted before they
graduate. Most American admissions officers believe the SAT, [15]
which tests a student's aptitude in basic verbal, math and reasoning skills rather than any particular mastery of high school course
content, improves their ability to predict which students may not
be able to deal with college course work. The SAT's ability to predict those students who will stay and those who will drop out in [20]
their freshman year has been studied by ETS and university re-
searchers, and their studies do suggest that scores on this test predict flunk-outs better than high school grades alone. The test also
evens out the varying grading standards that exist among American high schools. Since high school grades are weighted more [25]
than admissions test scores, this leveling function is useful.

When the SAT was first offered in 1926 it was not received so
enthusiastically. Only about eight thousand students chose to
take it that year, and eleven years later the number had increased
by only a thousand. The test was developed by the College En- [30]
trance Examination Board (usually just referred to as the "College
Board"), an organization that represented only thirty-five colleges when it was founded in 1900 but which now has a member-
ship composed of thousands of colleges, high schools and educational organizations. The College Board was created to standard- [35]

[12] a situation unimaginable in Japan : 学生が収容人数を越えてしまうからあまり「不可」をつけないでくれというプレッシャーを教師が受けるのは，うちの大学だけじゃないみたいですが，これは教師が日本的な寄合感覚で運営しているから起こる．アメリカでは大学の運営はそれ専門の人間がやっているわけで，みずから正しいと信じる基準で成績を出す教師の professional な仕事に口出しするというのは，逆に unimaginable なことになる．

[18] their ability : their は学生ではなく 15 行めの入学審査係 (admissions officers) を指す．

[20] stay : （留年する，ではなく）大学のカリキュラムについていく

[23] evens out the varying grading standards : さまざまに異なる成績の基準をならす．大学進学を前提に高度な教育を実施する私立の prep schools と公立高校との間の格差だけでなく，同じ public school でも，郊外の裕福な地域と，暴力や麻薬の問題の絶えない都市内奥部 (inner city) の学校との間には，同じ A の成績でも当然格差が出てくるわけ．

[25] are weighted more : より重視される

[26] leveling : evening-out

ize the college admission process for its members, and by 1907 it had developed achievement tests in English, French, German, Spanish, Latin, Classical Greek as well as math, physics, chemistry, botany, geography, history and drawing. That year they attracted only about a thousand test takers, even though they of- [5] fered the tests at sixty-seven cities in the U.S. and two in Europe which was much more convenient for students than traveling to each of the colleges to which they were applying for entrance examinations. And, of course, many professors liked the College Board's tests because they no longer had to write or score them — [10] something that most professors in Japan must do to this day. Those high school and college teachers who did these jobs for the College Board, and later for ETS, were paid for their work (as I have been since the sixties), and they could also enjoy all expense paid trips to New York and other places to perform them. [15]

Critics of the College Board's earlier achievement tests raised some of the same issues that are argued by critics of Japan's entrance examinations — that test success involves too much memorizing and too little reasoning and that test content dictates what is taught in high schools. Some colleges also felt that adopt- [20] ing the College Board's standardized admission tests threatened their own control over what they expected applicants to know, but no one complains about this anymore.

Use of the College Board's tests grew slowly until the 1920's when, influenced by the intelligence tests developed by the army [25] during World War I to identify potential officer material, they developed the SAT which was a real departure from their achievement tests. The Board thought "aptitude" was a more tactful word than "intelligence," but the intellectual potential that "IQ tests" attempt to measure is quite similar to the academic po- [30] tential that an aptitude test like the SAT claims to assess. Somehow the idea of aptitude testing struck a democratic chord in the hearts of college admissions people because, like the American Dream itself, it focused on future promise independent of past academic advantages or disadvantages. This interpretation, with [35]

[10] write : (入試問題を)作成する

[14] expense paid trips : 経費向こうもちの旅行

[15] perform them : do their jobs

[19] dictate(s) : 左右する

[22] their own control over what they expected applicants to know : つまり，「ウチの大学にくるならこれだけの知識はつけておきなさい」ということを，それぞれの大学で決定する自由.

[29] tactful : 「事の実体をうまく隠蔽する」というニュアンスあり.
intellectual potential : (将来どれだけ伸びる力を持っているかという意味での)知力.

[30] IQ : I は intelligence, Q は「指数」を意味する quotient.

[31] claims to assess : 測ることができるとうたっている

[32] struck a democratic chord in the hearts of : ～の心の中の民主主義を愛する気持に訴えた

[33] the American Dream : 基本的に階級社会であるヨーロッパとはちがってアメリカでは誰でも luck と pluck (がんばり) さえあれば丸太小屋からホワイトハウスにでものぼりつめることができるのだ，という信仰.

[34] promise : (成功の)見込み
independent of past academic advantages or disadvantages : これまでどの程度の教育を受けてこられたかということとは無関係に

[35] with a few twists to accomodate . . . : ～を考慮して若干の調整 (twists) を加えながら

a few twists to accommodate changing social circumstances, has
stuck to the SAT through World War II, the Cold War period, and
up through the Civil Rights and Affirmative Action movements.
Although the particular questions and problems posed by the
SAT change with every test administration, the test itself re- [5]
mained fundamentally the same (basic high school math, basic
vocabulary and other verbal and reasoning skills that can be
tested with multiple choice questions) until 1993. That year it was
revised to reflect the more conservative ideals that were gaining
favor not only in academic circles but in most aspects of Ameri- [10]
can life.

Today the SAT consists of two parts. The first, called "SAT-I:
Reasoning Tests" is very similar to the old SAT, and most selective colleges require their applicants to take it. Like the old SAT,
the SAT-I is made up of a verbal and a mathematical section, but [15]
the verbal section places more emphasis on reading critically than
the old test. Instead of asking multiple choice questions about
single passages, it includes double passages by different writers
expressing different points of view on the same topic. This requires more careful reading than the old one did, but the vocabu- [20]
lary testing may be easier since the words tested are drawn from
the reading passages. Test takers can take hints at their meaning
by seeing how the words are used in the passage. And the math
section emphasizes more interpretation of data and applied
mathematics than the problems on the old test, and now test [25]
takers may use their calculators. But it's the second part of the
new SAT called SAT-II that marks the greatest change. SAT-II
tests academic achievement in a variety of subjects in much the
same way that Japanese admission tests do. This year SAT-II tests
are available in eighteen different high school subjects: writing, [30]
literature, American history, world history, three levels of math,
three sciences, and eight languages. One of these languages is
Japanese which makes me think that the U.S. entrance test situation has just about reached the intensity it had in Japan when I
had my first experience with them over thirty years ago. [35]

[3] Civil Rights and Affirmative Action movements： 50年代から60年代にかけての「公民権運動」(Civil Rights movements) の目的は，特に学校や乗物・食堂などでの黒人差別の撤廃が焦点．その後70年代以降は，より積極的に(たとえば各大学が一定割合で黒人を入学させるというような)少数民族や女性の雇用・高等教育などを推進するAffirmative Actionへと運動の中心は変化していった．

[9] the more conservative ideals： 儒教的価値観を伝統とする日本とは正反対に，アメリカでは他人または社会の統制を振り切って，しゃにむに前進する「開拓者精神」が「保守的」な立場．画一的な客観テストからの脱却を声高に叫ぶのは，そうした保守勢力の方である．

[26] calculators： 現在アメリカの公立学校のほとんどでは，「もっとクリエイティブなことに時間と労力を使わせるべき」との基本的な考え方のもとに，算数の時間に電卓を使うことを奨励している．

[34] just about： だいたい．*Finished?—Just about.*

Questions 23-25
This is an ad posted on a bulletin board.

男子学生に部屋貸します．
南向きの四畳半．
東京大学から歩いて七分．
一か月四万円． 3811-7548

23. What is being advertised?
(A) Tutoring provided by a university student
(B) A vacancy for a roommate
(C) Room wanted by a male student
(D) A room for rent

24. How is the location described?
(A) As a 7-minute walk from the University of Tokyo
(B) As a 7-minute walk from Tokyo Station
(C) As a 7-minute ride from the University of Tokyo
(D) As a 7-minute train from Tokyo Station

25. What is the cost?
(A) 4,000 yen per month
(B) 4,000 yen per year
(C) 40,000 yen per month
(D) 40,000 yen per year

SATの「外国語」として日本語を選択することもできる．

A few years ago something like a *juku* opened for business in the office space just above the public library near my house. It began by offering tutoring and small classes for students having difficulty with course work in junior and senior high schools. Last year they added classes to prepare students for SAT examinations. This year I heard they were looking for a better location with more space for larger classes. Yes, it's beginning to seem a bit like Japan over here. [5]

Identifying Sentence Errors

Directions: The following sentences test your knowledge of grammar, usage, word choice, and idiom.

If there is an error, select the one underlined part that must be changed to make the sentence correct and fill in the corresponding oval on your answer sheet. If there is no error, fill in answer oval E.

1. Few people cannot hardly (A) tell (B) the difference between purple and fuchsia, even when (C) samples of these related colors are (D) placed side by side. No error (E)

2. The tallest (A) structure in the United States is (B) a television tower that raises (C) 2,063 feet above the plains (D) in Blanchard, North Dakota. No error (E)

3. Among the civilizations of the ancient world, that of the Romans are (A) far better (B) known to us (C) than any other (D). No error (E)

4. The commission investigating (A) the accident at the laboratory was less interested in why the experiment was conducted than in (B) whether they were (C) conducted properly (D). No error (E)

Yes, it's beginning to seem a bit like Japan . . . . （SAT新課程練習問題集より）
ちなみに答は，1—A，2—C，3—A，4—C.

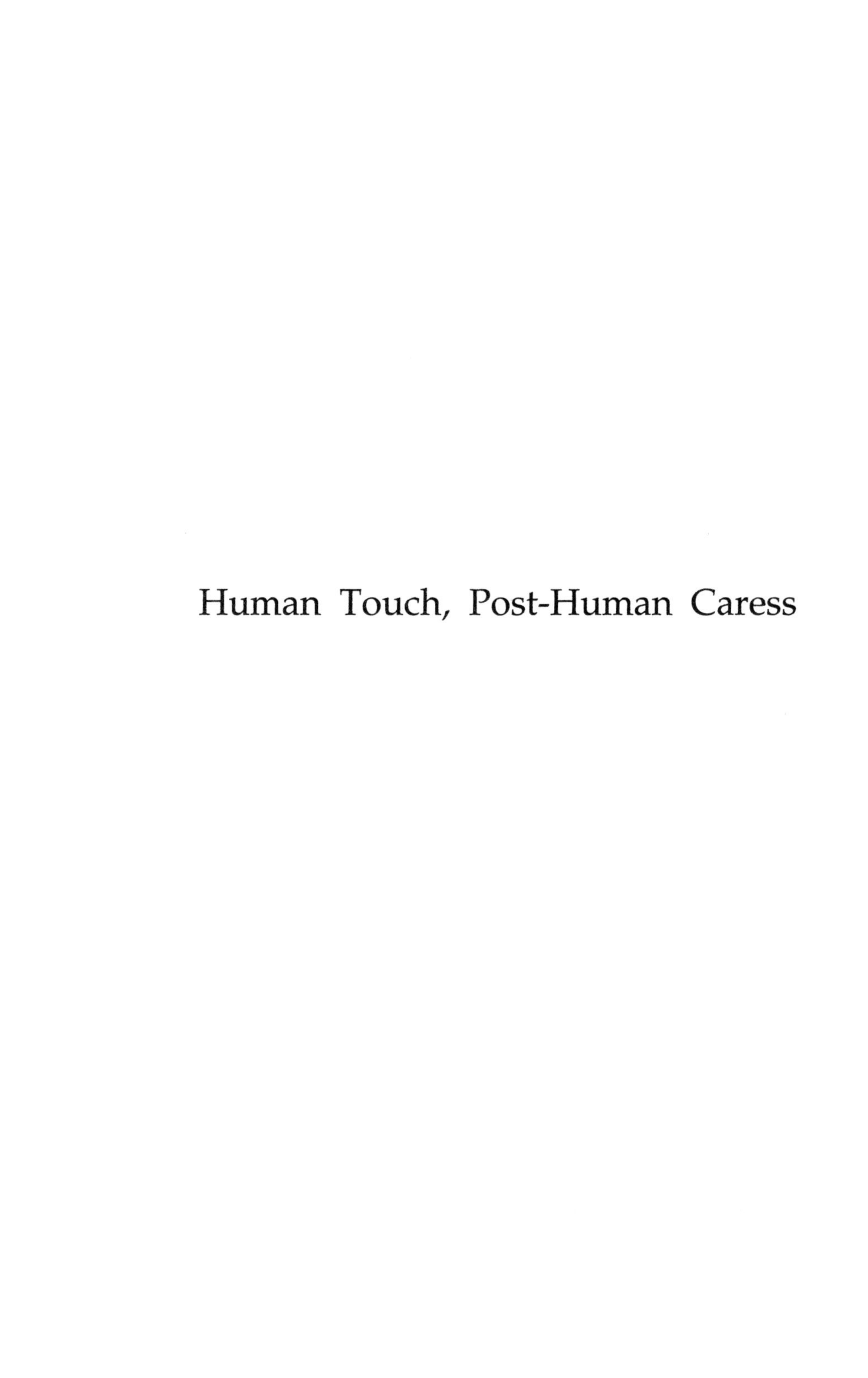

Human Touch, Post-Human Caress

1 2 3 4 5

SESSION 11

Hara Setsuko and the Art of Ozu Yasujirô

■

Mark Petersen

IN HIS 1949 MASTERPIECE *Banshun*, Ozu Yasujirô introduced to post-War Japan one of the most deeply felt, complexly realized, and dramatically satisfying characters he would ever create (or, for that matter, Hara Setsuko would ever play): Somiya Noriko. In one scene she would betray an oddly postpu- [5] bescent sort of "fastidiousness," and then, in a following scene, flirt confidently and in full control with a man eight years her senior. Still later, when a matronly "rival" appears to threaten the settled security of life with her father, she can suddenly stun us with the unexpected authority in her deep-set eyes, with an eerily [10] absolute will.

We are at once both frightened and attracted here: frightened by the uncompromising hardness we sense at her core, and attracted by the contrasting pliancy implied in her aura of sexual potential. In a sense, it is Hara Setsuko far more than Somiya [15] Noriko who affects us in this way. It is, in fact, nearly impossible for us today to picture Noriko as anyone *other* than Hara Setsuko. In a performance this pure, distinctions in persona between actress and acted tend to be blurred; if anything, we are now led rather in the *opposite* direction, back to envision the production of [20] the screenplay itself, to imagine Ozu and his collaborator Noda Kôgo sitting at a low table creating Noriko's lines with the image

マーク・ピーターセン氏は明治大学政治経済学部教授．俳句から現代アメリカ文学まで，あるいは映画からワインまでに至る幅広い知識と関心を，達意の日本語で軽妙洒脱に披露する．英語と日本語との違いをめぐる感度のよさは，名著『日本人の英語』『続日本人の英語』(岩波新書) などに十二分に発揮されている．●

[2] the most deeply felt . . . dramatically satisfying characters : "deeply felt" / "complexly realized" / "dramatically satisfying" の 3 つのペアがすべて characters にかかる．realize とは，あるキャラクターを具体的に表現すること．*This heroine is not a fully realized character.*

[4] for that matter : それをいえば，さらにいえば

[5] Somiya Noriko : 曾宮紀子．27 歳，大学教授の父(笠智衆(りゅうちしゅう))と 2 人で鎌倉に暮らしている．

she would betray an oddly postpubescent sort of "fastidiousness" : betray は(秘密，本音などを)「見せる，露呈する」．postpubescent は「すでに思春期を越えた」，"fastidiousness" は「潔癖さ，やかましさ」．歳に似合わぬ潔癖さの例については，次ページ 31～34 行目とその注を参照．

[7] flirt confidently and in full control with a man eight years her senior : flirt は日本語になりにくい言葉だが，くどくいえば，男女が，潜在的に恋愛関係・性的関係に陥る可能性があることをあたかも暗黙の前提にしているかのように親しげにふるまうこと．a man eight years her senior は父の助手の服部(宇佐美淳)．服部と紀子はたがいに憎からず思っているが，2 人の関係は成就しない．

[8] a matronly "rival" : matronly は「中年で品のある」．演じるのは三宅邦子．

[9] she can suddenly stun us . . . : stun は「唖然とさせる」．三宅邦子が父親の再婚候補であるらしいことが判明してからしばらく，我々は原節子の(ものすごく)怖い顔を見つづけることになる．

[10] deep-set : 深くくぼんだ

eerily : 不気味に

[13] uncompromising hardness : 妥協を知らない厳しさ

[14] pliancy : 柔順さ，しなやかさ

her aura of sexual potential : 隠れたセクシュアリティを感じさせるオーラ

[18] In a performance this pure : ここまで純粋な演技になると

[20] envision : to imagine visually

[21] his collaborator Noda Kôgo : 野田高悟．小津安二郎の主要作品ほとんどすべての脚本を書いた，撮影の厚田雄春とともに小津映画に不可欠の存在．

[22] lines : 科白

of Hara Setsuko herself, thick-featured and compelling, floating before them as they write.

It is also difficult for us today fully to appreciate what must have been the depth of Hara Setsuko's appeal. The exoticism of her "Western-style beauty," once the food of dreams, no longer [5] constitutes such a serious enticement, and the example of her very private, personal integrity no longer offers the same force of emotional encouragement. But to see the Hara Setsuko of *Banshun* in her true element — at the sea, in the open air, stretched out atop a dune, or bicycling along an empty coastal [10] roadway, radiantly full-faced and open to the wind — is surely to *begin* the process of appreciation. To this vibrant image we can contrast the grime and continuing hardship, the anxieties and daily frustrations experienced by most of the audiences that actually sat watching *Banshun* in the dreary movie theaters of 1949. [15]

Somiya Noriko was a twenty-seven-year-old woman who had, like so many others of her generation, been cheated of youth by the long war and its aftermath. She had contracted tuberculosis in "labor service" and endured whatever other injuries and indignities had to be endured by young women who wished to survive [20] those years. Yet, as we find her in *Banshun*, she has clearly managed to retain a portion of herself free of the contagion: pure, somehow, and unjaded by the inhumanity. This is the true source of her charisma in the film, of her ability in 1949 to inspire others who wished only to restart their lives with a similar pride. [25]

Hara Setsuko supplies much to the character of Noriko: the force of her own personality, of course, and a voice that seduces — and a huge, overwhelming smile which almost never seems to mean just happiness (note the frequent tension, the fleeting, nervous tautness of her upper lip whenever that smile cloaks an [30] emotion of special significance; as when, for example, she smilingly accuses the fifty-five-year-old Onodera, a friend of her father's, of "indecency" in having taken for a new wife a woman precisely her own age).

In later years, this colossal smile would mature — along with [35]

[1] thick-featured and compelling： ずんぐりした，存在感のある

[3] fully to appreciate： fully は appreciate にかかる．to fully appreciate でもよさそうに思えるが，そのように to と動詞が離れるのは「分離不定詞」(split infinitive) といって，折り目正しい英文では嫌われる傾向がある．

[6] constitute(s)： to form; make up. この単語は，たいていの場合 be 動詞と置き替えてもさほど意味は変わらない．

enticement： 魅惑

[7] personal integrity： 個人としての立派さ

offers the same force of emotional encouragement： 原節子演じるキャラクターが，当時は人々を「励ました」という点は，このあと詳しく述べられる．

[9] in her true element： いちばん自分らしさの出ている

[10] stretched out atop a dune： 砂丘の上にゆったり体を伸ばした

bicycling along . . .： 小野寺を「不潔よ」となじるときの笑顔(31 行目注を参照)とは違い，晴れた空を背にしたこのときの笑顔には本当に曇りがない．

[11] radiantly full-faced： ふっくらした顔 (full face) を燦然と輝かせた

[12] vibrant： 活気ある

[13] grime： 垢，汚れ

[15] dreary： 侘しい

[16] had . . . been cheated of youth： 若さをだまし取られた，不当に奪われた

[18] had contracted tuberculosis in "labor service"： 紀子は戦時中勤労動員に駆り出され，無理がたたって結核にかかった．映画のなかではほぼ回復しており，「お前，どうだったい，血沈？ / 15 に下がった / そうかい，そりゃよかった」という科白がある．

[19] endured whatever other injuries and indignities had to be endured by . . .： その他，～が耐えねばならなかったさまざまな傷や屈辱に耐えてきた

[22] retain： to keep; avoid losing

contagion： 文字どおりには「伝染」．ここでは戦争がもたらした一連の苦しみ・傷すべてを指している．

[23] unjaded： 鈍くなっていない，色あせていない

[24] charisma： カリスマ性

[27] seduce(s)： 誘惑する，魅する

[29] the frequent tension, the fleeting, nervous tautness of her upper lip whenever . . .： frequent tension は「頻繁に見られる緊張」．fleeting, nervous tautness は「つかのまの，苛立ったような引きつり」．

[30] cloak(s)： おおい隠す

[31] when . . . she smilingly accuses the fifty-five-year-old Onodera . . .： 「ねえおじ

the maturing of Hara's own spirituality — to intensify even further her screen presence and to lend to her already absorbing, tired-eyed, giant face something of an *Asuka Daibutsu* quality.

* * * * *

Ozu has apparently been criticized for being out of touch with "the real world." In *Banshun* — with its tea ceremony, shopping, and leisurely travels — there is in fact little to suggest any "postwar confusion." But Ozu was a genuine student of Hollywood and knew that desperate audiences responded just as meaningfully to offers of hope as to displays of added desperation. In *Banshun*, Ozu presented the example of people who were already living normally again, who had managed to restore to themselves an ordinary sense of dignity. In this he was simply advancing the heartening prospect that everyone might eventually accomplish the same thing. Hollywood had reacted to the Great Depression by showing the ridiculously rich at play in an opulent, imaginary Art Deco universe. For the most part, its audiences *did* achieve the intended escape and left the theater with, perhaps, a lingering sense that in a country capable of making such films prosperity was sure to be somewhere not too far around the corner. The difference between what Hollywood did then and what Ozu did in 1949 was simply that Ozu was significantly more restrained in his execution. His equivalent of the immense Art Deco set was the occasional use of a spacious, brightly lit, very modern Ginza coffee shop, and in place of the futuristic promise of familiar American skyscrapers like the Chrysler Building, Ozu gave us, as a backdrop, the enduring anchor of the Wakô Building.

And also at his artistic disposal, to demonstrate that people might not only be human again but actually wonderful again, Ozu had Hara Setsuko. Other directors occasionally had Hara Setsuko at their disposal, too, but none ever used her to the same lasting effect.

* * * * *

さま / ん？/ おじさまね / 何だい / 奥様おもらいになったんですってね / うん，もらったよ / 美佐子さん(小野寺の娘)がお可哀想だわ / どうして / だって，やっぱり変じゃないかしら / そうでもなさそうだよ，うまくいってるらしいよ / そうかしら．でも，何だか嫌ね / 何が，今度の奥さんかい / ううん，おじさまがよ / どうして / 何だか不潔よ / 不潔 . . . / 汚ならしいわ / 汚ならしい . . . (笑)ひどいことになったな，汚ならしいか(お手ふきで顔を拭いて)どうだい / 駄目駄目 / そうかい，駄目かい，これは困ったな / はい(お酌する) / そうかい，不潔かい / そうよ / そりゃあ弱ったな」．原節子はここで一貫してニコニコしているが，なんとなく怖い．

[35] colossal : 巨大な，途方もない

[13] heartening prospect : (見る者を)勇気づける展望

[14] the Great Depression : 大恐慌．1929 年 10 月の株式大暴落にはじまった世界的事態をいう．

[15] opulent : extremely rich

[16] Art Deco universe : 「アール・デコ風の宇宙」．昔のハリウッド映画に出てくる，それこそ「デコデコ」した派手なセットを思い浮かべればいい．

[18] prosperity was sure to be . . . around the corner : prosperity (繁栄，好景気) が around the corner (すぐそこまで来ている) というのは一種の定型句．*the too-ready optimism which continues to assert that prosperity is just around the corner* (好景気はすぐそこまで来ていると相も変わらず主張する，あまりに安易な楽天)

[21] Ozu was significantly more restrained in his execution : そうした希望を与えるやり方 (execution) において，小津の方がずっと抑制が利いていた

[22] equivalent : 同等物，対応物

[24] the futuristic promise of . . . the Chrysler building : 1930 年に完成し，現在もエンパイア・ステート・ビル以上の人気を誇るクライスラー・ビルは，同時期に作られた未来映画『メトロポリス』の世界にも通じる外見をもち，当時の未来像を雄弁に具現しているように思える．

[26] the enduring anchor of the Wakô Building : 永く変わらぬ錨(のように安定した存在)として，銀座 4 丁目の和光ビルはいまも健在．

[27] at his artistic disposal : 芸術家として彼が使える，手中にしている．*My library is totally at your disposal.* (書斎をどうぞご自由にお使い下さい)

「麦秋」小津安二郎監督　1951（昭和 26）年　松竹株式会社

「東京物語」小津安二郎監督　1953（昭和 28）年　松竹株式会社

（上）「晩春」小津安二郎監督
1949（昭和 24）年
（下）「秋刀魚の味」小津安二郎
監督 1962（昭和 37）年
いずれも松竹株式会社

Somiya Noriko comes to us in *Banshun* fully three-dimensional; it is Ozu's particular artistic genius to take her one step further, to let us explore Noriko along a *fourth* dimension by depicting variants of her persona in subsequent films. In *Bakushû* (1951) Somiya Noriko has become Mamiya Noriko, and her household is comprised of an extended, three-generation family. There is an openness and airiness to this home, and a broadness to its humor. Nothing so perfectly symbolizes the fundamental contrast of atmospheres in *Bakushû* and *Banshun* as does the balancing of the famous Noh scene in *Banshun* with the Kabuki scene in *Bakushû*. This parallel is a precise reflection of just how the two films diverge in both flavor and ambition.

Mamiya Noriko is a year older now, and as is signified in the progression of film titles from *Banshun* to *Bakushû* (from *Late Spring* to *Early Summer*), she has advanced one more year beyond the ideal marriage age. She has outgrown any odd "fastidiousness," if indeed she had ever had any, and now, with a mother, older brother, sister-in-law, and two nephews in the same home, there is little room for any intensity in the relationship she has with her father. She is working, and she makes an important contribution to the family income. The old Noriko "pride" is there, the same solid sense of identity, but what has evolved in this new setting is a posture of independence. Her decision to reject a recommended arranged marriage in favor of a superficially less advantageous union with Yabe is, among other things, a direct assertion of that independence. When, in *Bakushû*, Noriko is with her friend Aya, we are reminded of a similarly girlish playfulness that she occasionally displayed in *Banshun* (also with a friend named Aya), but the playfulness in *Bakushû* is far more lighthearted: the old Noriko, unlike the new, would never ever have been encouraged to creep up to a second floor *ozashiki* to spy on *anyone*, much less to sneak a glimpse of a forty-year-old suitor she had recently rejected, sight unseen, in defiance of her family's wishes.

The evolution of Noriko is completed in *Tôkyô Monogatari*. Here

[3] by depicting variants of her persona in subsequent films : その後の映画で，紀子というキャラクターのさまざまなバリエーションを描くことによって

[5] Mamiya Noriko : 間宮紀子．28 歳，専務秘書．

[6] an extended, three-generation family : 3 世代にわたる拡大家族

[7] broadness : 大らかさ

[9] the balancing of the famous Noh scene in *Banshun* . . . : 『晩春』では紀子が父と2 人で能を見にいき，『麦秋』では田舎から上京してきた親類が紀子の両親と一緒に歌舞伎を見にいく．能のシーンは長く緊張に満ち，歌舞伎のシーンは和やかで短い．

[11] diverge in both flavor and ambition : 趣においても，目指していることにおいてもはっきり方向が分かれる

[16] has outgrown : ～を卒業してしまっている

[19] there is little room for . . . : ～の余地はほとんどない

[20] she makes an important contribution to the family income : ある日など紀子は900 円(昭和 26 年で!)のショートケーキを買ってきて，兄嫁(三宅邦子)らと一緒に食べる．

[23] a posture of independence : 独立の姿勢

[24] arranged marriage : 見合い結婚

in favor of a superficially less advantageous union with Yabe : 「矢部(二本柳寛)との，表面的には劣る結婚を選んで」．兄嫁が紀子に，矢部と結婚したらもうケーキも食べられなくなる，と冗談まじりに言うシーンもある．「もう食べちゃ駄目よ，ショートケーキ / 当たり前よ，あんな高いもの．でももらったら食べる．ウフフ」

[25] among other things : なかでも，特に

[27] Aya : 田村アヤ(淡島千景)，料亭の娘．

[28] also with a friend named Aya : こちらは北川アヤ(月丘夢路)，タイピスト(「タイピストって言うんじゃないのよ，ステノグラファーよ」)．結婚経験者．

[31] encouraged to creep up : creep up は「こっそりのぼっていく」．そうするよう紀子を encourage するのは，料亭の娘アヤ．

[32] sneak a glimpse of . . . : ～を盗み見る

a forty-year-old suitor : 40 歳の花婿候補．小津映画では，娘の結婚相手が登場しないことが多いが(『晩春』でも，紀子の結婚相手の佐竹熊太郎，34 歳，東大理科卒，丸の内の日東化成勤務，実家は伊予の松山の旧家，は叔母たちが噂するだけで画面には登場しない)，この花婿候補もやはり画面には現われない．

[33] sight unseen : 見もせずに

[35] *Tôkyô Monogatari* : 『東京物語』(1953)．ここで論じられているほかの小津映画

she is a war widow; her married name is Hirayama Noriko. Ozu has moved us along again in the fourth dimension to reveal other aspects of her persona, other might-have-beens for other years in other circumstances. Her suffering this time has been more profound and her maturity is now fully achieved. Near the end of [5] *Tôkyô Monogatari*, Noriko breaks down in front of her father-in-law. She weeps, she confides her loneliness, her deepest sadnesses, her fears. The scene is all the more moving because we understand that now, except for this old man, there is no one else in the world to whom she can possibly speak so honestly. [10]

* * * * *

The last view of Noriko in *Tôkyô Monogatari* shows her aboard a train that leaves Onomichi to disappear forever, and the Noriko persona that we have been following here disappears with her. Something to remind us, however, is to be found in Ozu's very last film, *Sanma no Aji* (1962). The plot itself is a startling return to [15] *Banshun*, but the Japan we find in *Sanma no Aji* is changed. It has become, among other things, a society now fully enough recovered to suit the lucent tones of the Agfa-Shochikucolor in which Ozu has come to work — he no longer films in black and white.

The purest parallel to *Banshun* occurs near the end of the film, [20] when we repeat the scene of the father in black cutaway going upstairs to find his daughter seated, before a mirror, in a wedding kimono. Two things are particularly remarkable here. Unlike in *Banshun*, in this film Ryû Chishû abruptly cuts off the traditional *aisatsu* that his daughter is about to make; and the daughter, a [25] twenty-one-year-old Iwashita Shima, is so astonishingly lovely in kimono that we are forced to recall how lovely Hara Setsuko was *not*.

We may remember the great sadness of that last sight of Noriko in *Banshun*, and attribute the depth of the mood to the depth of [30] Noriko's continuing reluctance to become a bride. But viewed again, especially in contrast to *Sanma no Aji*, we realize that a part of the poignancy of the scene results from how poorly the formal

3本とは違って，娘が嫁に行く物語ではなく，尾道から上京してきた老いた両親（笠智衆，東山千栄子）と，その子供たちとのやりとりをめぐる話．

[1] Hirayama Noriko： 平山紀子．

[3] might-have-beens： そうなっていたかもしれない，別の彼女．この場合はそうではないが，後悔の念を表わすときに使われることが多い言葉．Cf. "My name is Might-have-been; / I am also called No-more, Too-late, Farewell." Dante Gabriel Rosetti, *Sonnets from the House of Life* (1870–1881).

[6] her father-in-law： 笠智衆．義理の娘である原節子は，実の子供たちよりはるかに彼らに優しい．

[7] she confides her loneliness, her deepest sadnesses . . .： 「わたくし，いつまでもこのままじゃいられないような気がするんです．このままこうして1人でいたら，いったいどうなるんだろうなんて，夜中にふと考えたりすることがあるんです．1日1日が何事もなく過ぎていくのが，とってもさみしいんです．どこか心の隅で，何かを待ってるんです．ずるいんです / いやあ，ずるうはない / いいえ，ずるいんです．そういうこと，お義母さまには申し上げられなかったんです / ええんじゃよ，それで．やっぱりあんたはええ人だよ．正直で / とんでもない」

[15] startling： surprising; unexpected

[18] the lucent tones of the Agfa-Shochikucolor： lucent は「澄んだ」．小津映画がカラーになったのは，1958年の『彼岸花』から．

[19] films： ここは「(映画を)撮る」という動詞．

[21] cutaway： モーニング

[31] Noriko's continuing reluctance to become a bride： 紀子が依然としてお嫁に行きたがっていないこと

[33] poignancy： 痛ましさ

Japanese bridal wear reflects Hara Setsuko's "Western-style beauty." The incompatibility of her very look evokes a kind of pathos. And when she kneels before her father and draws out those most traditional of final lines so very slowly, with long, painful pauses, "*Otôsan . . . nagai aida . . . iroiro . . . osewa ni narimashita . . . ,*" we feel an extra pain in watching her, a kind of pain that Ozu Yasujirô never again attempted to evoke with Hara Setsuko or any other actress. [5]

[2] incompatibility : 矛盾，両立しないこと

[3] pathos : 悲哀

SESSION 12

The Art of Romance Writing in America

■

Derek Pell

AHH, ROMANCE! . . . Ahh, America! . . . Ahh-choo!!! Excuse me, I have a bad cold. Whenever I suffer the slings and arrows of a seasonal flu, my mind becomes clouded, and I find myself in a state quite receptive to the joys of writing about romance in America. In fact, I'm somewhat of an expert on the [5] subject because, (a) I'm an American; (b) I fell in love with my wife via the Postal Service; (c) I have yet to learn the alphabet; (d) I am working on a book called *Weird Romance*.

As a teen-aged poet, I wrote my fair share of muck — half-baked haiku and over-priced free-verse — silly scribblings done [10] in an attempt to win the hearts (if not the minds) of girls I longed for. Unfortunately, I learned a cruel truth as a tender teen . . . Americans, by and large, *do not like poetry*. Thus, some of my best love-sick odes wound up in waste-baskets at school, tossed away so heartlessly by females rushing off to watch the other boys play [15] baseball.

Ahh, youth!

Oddly enough, such rejections didn't stop me from writing. Thankfully there was a war going on and I was able to vent my passions writing poems against the madness. But looking back on [20] those dusty years (circa 1965), I feel my time might have been better off had I sat down and written a "romance novel." I don't be-

永遠の60年代野郎，冗談のアートに命をかける不屈のパフォーマー，デレク・ペルは過去25年，作家としてビジュアル・アーティストとして，パロディ精神と病的ユーモア一本やりの作品群を発表し続けてきた．中には『ドクトル・ベイのセックス・ガイド』(1978)のように2万部さばいた本もあったけれど，レーガンとヤッピーの80年代に入ってからは出版界・美術界の反応は冷たくなった．それでも彼は今日もまた，ダークな感覚をとぎすまし，鈍重な日常性の破壊工作に余念がない．ぼくがサンディエゴを離れるときに，FOUCAULT-TEXT®という登録商標入りの「ポストモダン・タンポン」の箱をプレゼントしてくれた．㋚

[1] Ahh-choo!!!： くしゃみのオノマトペ(擬音語)．相手がくしゃみをしたら "Bless you!" といってあげるのが礼儀．こっちも，くしゃみの擬音です．

[2] slings and arrows： 風邪のひどいのにかかると，本当に石や矢が飛んでくる感じかどうかは，まあともかくとして....

[6] I'm an American： アメリカ人はロマンチックか？ 文学史的にいうと，ロマンスこそアメリカ的な形式だった．実社会の人間模様を緻密なプロットで描くノヴェルの形式は，荒野と文明が激しくぶつかるこの国ではなかなか育たなかったのだ．ホーソンの『緋文字』も，メルヴィルの『白鯨』も，想像力が思いっきり時空をかけめぐるロマンスだった——という話はここではあまり関係ない？

[7] via the Postal Service： デレクと奥さんのシーラとがペンパルとして知り合い，長年の文通の末に初めて会ってそのまま結婚にゴールインしたというのは，2人を知る人のあいだで今もよく語り草になる，ウソのようなホントの話です．
yet to learn the alphabet： どさくさにまぎれて，すぐこういうナンセンスを混ぜるんだから....

[9] wrote my fair share of muck： 私もご他聞にもれず下らぬものをよく書いた

[10] over-priced free-verse： 現代詩人は韻律にこだわらない「自由詩」を書き，それは「芸術的」といわれて『ニューヨーカー』などの雑誌に高く買われる．その手の意味のない作品を自分も若い頃には書いていたっけなあ——という感慨のこもる表現．

[11] if not the minds： heartが情の中枢ならmindは知の器官．mindを勝ち得ることができない，というのは，より直接的にいえばアホな詩だったということです．

[14] odes： 特定の人(や物事)を讃えたり追悼したりする叙情詩

[19] vent my passions writing poems against the madness： 反戦の詩を書いて(詩作への)情熱を発散させる

[21] dusty years (circa 1965)： 1948年生まれのデレクは当時高校生．circa [sə́rkə] は年数につけて「約」を意味する．dustyは「埃をかぶった」．

lieve the genre was as pervasive then as now, but it's a fact of life that women *love* romantic fiction. Of course, it's a lot easier to write a one-paged poem praising the female form, than to produce a hefty, 300-paged romantic saga. Besides, in a novel one has to deal with characters and plot and — oh no! — complete sen- [5] tences!

Ahh, *Gone with the Wind!*

Do not misunderstand me, I am not now, nor was I ever, a fan of romantic fiction, i.e., I'm far too cynical to believe that anything turns out well in the end. [10]

"And they lived happily ever after."

Oh, yeah? My own ending would go something like this: And they lived happily ever after, *alas.*

That, of course, is the job of the satirist, to find the crack in the rainbow's facade. Thus, I approached my *Weird Romance* with a [15] crooked sneer, stroking my villainous mustache like a pet python. But I soon found out that the job would not be simple. After reading several novels in the genre, it was clear to me that it would be hard to make them any more absurd than they already were. For example, how was I to improve on a passage as awk- [20] ward as this:

The washing machine went into the spin cycle and began walking, across the floor. "Chaos," he said, then grinned. Cruel word. Too easily spoken too easily used and abused, even by the innocent man who reigned it on her without thought of how barren she would be without it. [25] *She rolled her head away.*

The first sentence alone was astonishing. Indeed, it was worthy of a second-rate science fiction novel. The rest was pure gibberish, all reigning words and rolling heads, much like the work of some forgotten Surrealist poet. Perhaps that was it! I would pluck all [30] the queer non-sequiturs from a dozen such novels and string them together into a single, slithering text. Prose that only a monster could love, a collage of nouns and verbs and hundreds of trite

[21] better off : richer; more meaningful

[3] praising the female form : 恋人をたたえるヘボ詩はよく，「君の瞳は . . . 君の髪は . . . 」となります．

[4] hefty : heavy and bulky
saga : [sɑ́:gə] 家族何代にも渡って描かれるような大河小説

[12] Oh, yeah? : 「あーそーかい」．人に反論するときの，ちょっぴりケンカ腰の返答．

[14] to find the crack in the rainbow's facade : 虹といえば幸福の象徴．そんなロマンチックな見せかけ（facade [fəsɑ́:d]）のなかに，アラを見いだすこと

[16] crooked sneer : 悪意をたたえた冷笑
like a pet python : mustache [mʌ́stæʃ] の不気味さを際だたせるためとはいえ，大蛇とは派手な比喩だ．

[22] *The washing machine . . .* : 以下の文，デレクの創作（たぶんいくつかの文章からのコラージュ）．こういう，文章のようであってほとんど意味をなさない，腐乱した言葉の塊のようなものに，この作家は変わらぬ愛を抱いている．

[25] *reigned it on her* : reign（統治する）という語はふつうこうは使わない．同音の rained it on her なら「カオスという言葉を雨のように浴びせかける」の意味になる．
without thought of how barren she would be without it : こういう言葉を投げつけられることが彼女の人生の救いになっている，ってことなんでしょう．

[26] *rolled her head away* : eyes ならグリグリと roll することもできるけど . . . . 頭を「ゴロゴロ向こうに転がす」となると，もはやオカルトの世界．

[28] pure gibberish : total nonsense

[29] all reigning words and rolling heads : 言葉が reign したり頭がゴロゴロしたり，そんなのばっかり．

[30] Perhaps that was it! : そうか，たぶんそのやり方で（昔のシュールレアリスム風に）いけばいいんだ！（it に強勢がおかれる．）

[31] non-sequitur(s) : 理論的に結び合わない文

[32] a single, slithering text : 1本の蛇のようになめらかに這っていく文章

[33] trite : banal, unoriginal, too common

adjectives. I would sift through the mud and scoop up all the corn and clichés and stir them up in a giant cauldron, bubbling with bile.

So that is how I began my project. After filling a thick notebook with my booty, I realized that something more was needed [5] ... but what? Oh yes, I'd left out characters and plot. Here I was with stacks of crazed dialogue like:

You want to know what I'm afraid of? I'll tell you what I'm afraid of. I'm afraid of this fear . . . this fear that keeps building up inside me like a monster. A monster that makes me need you when I'd rather not, but [10] *can't fight it. And hell, I don't know if I've got the strength to pick up the pieces if I ever let myself get close to somebody else, and then if it doesn't work . . . falls apart like another house of cards . . . I can't face living surrounded by the evidence of the lousy, rotten hand life dealt me. Yeah, I'm a joker all right . . . a clown . . . but can't you see your clown is cry-* [15] *ing?*

There was enough of this nonsense to last me a lifetime, but I needed real, flesh and blood, human beings. I needed *Everycouple*! A girl and boy that would represent American youth. First, they needed typical American names. What should I call him? [20] Elvis? . . . Tarzan? . . . Akbar? And what would I call her? Zsa-Zsa? . . . Pia? . . . Farrah? . . . No, that was all wrong. I finally chose Wanda and Dexter. These names seemed to capture the spirit of restless youth, the sort of teens you'll find hanging out at MacDonald's or the local bowling alley. As for plot, I came up [25] with a rather twisted one. Since much of the "romance" in these books seemed alien to natural life, vaguely aquatic and devouring, I decided to loosely base my tale on the best-selling novel *Jaws*. There would, however, be no actual sharks in my story, only human ones who, in the end, devour themselves on the beach in a [30] tastefully rendered scene of cannibalism.

Now before you accuse me of being grotesque, let me remind you that I was satirizing a genre that produced descriptions such

[1] sift through the mud： 泥(みたいな文章)をふるいにかける
corn： (俗) something considered trite, dated, melodramatic, or unduly sentimental. "corny" (ダサイ，田舎っぽい) という形容詞形で戦前からよく使われた.

[2] bubbling with bile： 大鍋 (cauldron) の中に，胆汁を入れてぐつぐつ煮るというのは，魔女のイメージ.

[5] booty： 戦利品 (= all the corn and cliché)

[7] crazed dialogue： 感情が先走って支離滅裂になった会話文

[8] この文章を日本語に訳して，それを日本語の学習者が辞書を頼りに英語に訳してみたらどんな文ができるだろう，とデレクは考えた．で，ぼくの逐語訳と，知り合いのアメリカ人学生で実際やってみたのだけど，結果はいまいちでした.

[9] *I'm afraid of this fear*： afraid していることが fear の状態なのであって，fear が恐い，のではないのだけど，感情で喋っている人は実際こういう言い方もする.
building up： つもりつもっていく

[11] *can't fight it*： 抑えようにも抑えられない
hell： ヤケになってることを示すののしり言葉.
pick up the pieces： 責任をもって事を始末する

[12] *get close to somebody else*： 誰か別の女に近づくことを言っているのでしょう.

[13] *house of cards*： トランプで作った家．すぐにバラバラに崩れ落ちてしまうものの代表．*another* はここでは just another (よくその辺にある)の意味.

[14] *rotten hand life dealt me*： 人生が自分に配った，ひどい「手」．次の行にかけてトランプの比喩が一人歩きしている.

[17] to last me a lifetime： 一生かかっても使いきれない

[18] *Everycouple*： 15, 6 世紀イギリスの morality play (勧善懲悪の寓意劇) 以来 Everyman という名の「ふつう人」を登場させる物語が少なくないが，言われてみれば，ラブ・ロマンスなんてたいていが "Everycouple" の物語だ.

[21] Akbar： どんな名前をもってくるのかと思ったら，ムガール帝国の皇帝か！
Zsazsa： ツァツァといえば，むかし，ハンガリーからアメリカに渡ったツァツァ・ガボアという女優がいた．引用句事典で「結婚」とか「男」とかの項を引くと，彼女の機知に富んだ言葉がのっている.

[27] vaguely aquatic and devouring： シャワーやジャグジーの中での熱い抱擁とかいうのを想像するとわかる気がする.

[31] rendered： handled; described

as this:

> *Why couldn't he get her out of his head? His reaction to her wasn't logical, and was driving him crazy. The color-coordinated wardrobe hanging in his closet was practical. Running to keep his weight down was practical. In fact, everything in his life was practical. And that was precisely the way he liked it. Shirley, of course, was none of these things. She topped the list as the most impractical, unreasonable, disorderly woman he had ever known.*

So you see, cannibalism seems a fair penalty to fit the crime. Heck, *my* characters were getting off easy. At least they wouldn't be around to suffer through a sequel. Yet why blame the poor characters? After all, they didn't invent themselves and force their silly stories into the bookstores. No, it was the authors of these unspeakable books who deserved punishment.

When I had finished my masterpiece I was still not satisfied. The book was certainly strange and funny, but no more so than the real thing. It needed something else. It needed *pictures* — especially in light of the fact that my novel had to compete with actual romances as well as Soap Operas on TV. This would be the fun part of the project since I was not only skilled in the art of bad writing, but I also possessed a talent for visual collage. Computer graphics would be the perfect companion to *Weird Romance*. All I needed to do was find the appropriate (copyright free) images to manipulate. These were available in old encyclopedias and odd scientific books. I spent several months joyously performing surgery on photographs, and finally wedded them to my glorious text. The rest, as they say, is history.

That's not quite true, for the book has yet to see publication. To make matters worse, I began thinking about sequels, putting the old cart before the hearse. The one thing that most struck me about the romance genre was how absurdly alike a typical author's works were.

I was off on another romantic adventure. I would now invent a

[2] *couldn't . . . get her out of his head*: 彼女のことが心から離れない

[9] cannibalism seems a fair penalty to fit the crime: こんなアホなことで悩んだりしているヤツは食われてしまってもいい，ということ．

[10] Heck: hell（前ページ11行目の注参照）の一変形．

getting off easy: not suffering severe punishment

wouldn't be around to suffer through a sequel: シリーズになって次もまた登場なんてことにはならないので，その分苦しみも軽い，ということ．

[14] unspeakable: 言うもおぞましい

[17] the real thing: 「本物」とは，実際世に出回っているハーレクインなどのロマンスのこと．

[18] in light of: considering

[19] Soap Operas on TV: 「昼メロ」はテレビ以前にはラジオでやっていた．視聴者のほとんどが女性だからと，よく石鹸会社がスポンサーについたことがこの呼び名の由来．アメリカでもやはり「昼」にやるのがふつうだが，大金持ちの屋敷を舞台に策謀渦巻く *Dallas* や *Dynasty* の物語は夜のゴールデン・タイムを10年間も高視聴率で占領していた．どちらも世界各国に輸出されてヒット，日本でだけ鳴かず飛ばずだった．この手の話は，何回か見逃しても筋が解らなくなってしまうことはないはずなのだが，アメリカのマーケットのレジには *Soap Opera Digest* という雑誌がおいてあって，これを見れば，いつでもフォローできる．

[21] visual collage: こちらの方でデレクは，Norman Conquest（ノルマン人の征服）の名で仕事をしている．たとえば，*3 de Sade*（3Dのマルキ・ド・サド）という作品は，『ジュスティーヌ』の古書に錆びた釘が打ち込まれ，そこからドス黒い血が流れているというもの．このごろのコンピュータ・グラフィックスは，これほどグロくはないですけどね．

[25] performing surgery on photographs: グラフィック・ソフトの〈distort〉メニューなどを使って，変形手術を施すのが主な方法．カラーの口絵を見てください．

[27] The rest, as they say, is history: 有名人が自分の出世話などを語るとき，「あとはみなさんよくご存じの通り」という意味あいで，"The rest is history" とよくいうのをもじった，ややマゾヒスティックともとれる冗談．

[29] putting the old cart before the hearse: hearse（霊柩車）じゃなくて horse だと「物事の順番が逆」，「辻褄があわない」という意味の慣用句になるんですが....

romance novel author — Rosemary Sage! — and create a book of paperback covers that would comprise her "collected works."

The following selection is from my introduction to *The Collected Works of Rosemary Sage:*

Who but Rosemary Sage could have written the novel Defiled [5] Heights *(1980). Her words, her inimitable style, have become the hallmarks of modern romantic literature. Her uncanny sense of sentence structure, timing, non-sequitur, is as uniquely her own as the tantalizing plots she so skillfully constructs in her heart-shaped bathtub. Her voice is a rare one; it drifts above the over-crowded choir and haunts the* [10] *air like a bird that has forgotten how to fly.*

Each year, thousand of lesser talents attempt to imitate her, to capture that rare "Sag-ian" quality, yet never succeed, for a novel by Rosemary Sage is not simply a work of fiction . . . it is an out-of-body experience. *And that, in part, explains why her name is a household word in nearly* [15] *every household in America and a dozen other countries as well. Her books are beloved by heads of state, housewives, inmates, and Hollywood stars. Although she is scorned by critics who blithely label her books "mindless trash," she pays no attention — listens only to the millions of adoring fans. In fact, she receives so many fan letters and gifts addressed* [20] *to her home in Lodi, New Jersey that the local post office was forced to open an annex just to house all her mail.*

It's not so surprising when you consider that she has written over 60 books and sold more than 300 million copies. But what is truly remarkable is that she spends eight months out of every year on promotional [25] *tours arranged by her publishers. Furthermore, she holds the world's record for the most books signed in a day (4,006). Alas, due to a severe case of carpal tunnel syndrome, Ms. Sage is now forced to dictate her inscriptions.*

Unfortunately, I cannot present the 60 cover illustrations which [30] follow the introduction. Still, it should prove instructive if I list a few of her titles: *Defile Me, My Love; Defile Me Not; A Bride Defiled; Return To Defiled Aisle; Dial Defiled; Redial Defiled; Return of the*

[1] Rosemary Sage： イギリス古謡で，サイモンとガーファンクルの歌で知られる"Scarborough Fair" の歌詞に，"Parsley, sage, rosemary and thyme" と，ハーブの名前が連なるところがあったけど.... とにかくもろにフェミニンで(Rosemary) しかも作家先生っぽくて (Sageは「賢人」という意味)，さらにばかばかしい組み合わせ，というのがねらい.

[5] Defiled Heights： *Wuthering Heights* が「嵐が丘」なら，これは何と訳すべきか.「ケガレが丘」？「恥辱の丘」？ 陰湿にエッチな響きがほしいところだ.

[7] *uncanny sense of*...： 本の宣伝文句などで「神がかり的に鋭い」という意味で多用されるフレーズだけれど，uncanny はもともとは「不気味」という意味．以下，この手の「意味の二重映し」が続いていく.

[9] *heart-shaped bathtub*： 恋愛小説の作家女史の家のお風呂ってこうなのか！1950年代のナイアガラ・フォールズは，新婚旅行のメッカで，ホテルにはよくこういうのがあったそうですが.... 日本のラブモテル事情は知りません.

Her voice is a rare one： 「とびきりの一級品」という常套句の意味が，次の具体的記述によって貶められる．たしかに「珍しい」声のようだ.

[10] *the over-crowded choir*： 無数の作家がロマンチックにさえずっているたとえ.

[14] out-of-body experience： 魂が肉体を抜け出す超常現象．作家の魂がそのまま本になって出てきたなんて，気持わるーい.

[15] *her name is a household word*： 知名度・浸透度をいうときの常套句． たしかにローズマリーやセージは，どの家の台所でも聞かれる言葉ですが....

[17] *heads of state*： 国家元首

[21] *Lodi*： [lóudai] どこか丘の上か海岸べりの高級住宅地を想像したらお生憎様．ここはマンハッタンに近いニュージャージーの工場町です.

[28] *carpal tunnel syndrome*： 「手根管症候群」といって，手や指に痛みや異常感覚を覚える病気.

[32] *Defile Me, My Love*： 以下 "Defile" の訳語としては「犯す」がお勧め.

[33] *Dial Defiled*： ちなみに，"Dial" で始まる恐怖映画に，モデルさんの部屋にこわーい電話が鳴りつづける *Dial Help* というのがあった．(この電話には悪霊が乗り移っていて，彼女はレイプされてしまう....)

Return of the Defiled： "Return of" をつけるのは，連作の題名の基本形．「蠅男」も「キラー・トマト」も「リヴィング・デッド」も「ピンク・パンサー」も，ブルース・リーの「ドラゴン」も――そういえばウルトラマンも――みんな「帰ってきた」.

Defiled; Defiled, Ahoy!; Defiled On Trial; Defiled Days; Defiled Nights; Defiled Day and Night; Reviled, Beguiled & Defiled; Once in Awhile Defiled; Defiled On the Nile; Defiled in Style; A Miler Defiled; Smile, My Defiled; and Remembrance of Defilement's Past.

Now you can understand why we call Rosemary Sage "the queen of hysterical romance." It is even rumored that Ms. Sage is at work on her first cookbook, tentatively titled *The Defiled Chef.* [5]

As for me, well, I've got to find a publisher for my *Weird Romance* since my wife has threatened to divorce me if I don't. I think that pretty much sums up what romance writing in America is all about. A dirty job . . . but somebody simply has to do it. [10]

[1] *Defiled, Ahoy!*: Ahoy! という呼びかけは，かつて船乗りが使った．“Ship Ahoy!”で「おーい，その船ー!」という感じ．「汚された女」を呼び止めるには，あまりにアホい？

Defiled On Trial: 「裁かれる Defiled」．このあたり，Defiled という言葉がほとんど固有名詞化している．

[2] *Reviled, Beguiled & Defiled*: 「あざけられ，あざむかれ，おかされて」．往年のイタリア映画に「誘惑されて棄てられて」というのがあったけど....

[3] *Defiled On the Nile*: *Death on the Nile* といえば，アガサ・クリスティの小説名．このあたり，*Smile, My Defiled* まで脚韻を基準としたリストが続く．

Miler: 長距離ランナー

[4] *Remembrance of Defilement's Past*: プルーストの小説『失われた時を求めて』の英題は *Remembrance of Things Past.*

[10] pretty much: かなりのところまで

what romance writing in America is all about: アメリカでロマンスを書くということが一体どんなことか

[11] A dirty job . . . but somebody simply has to do it: 大学の教養の英語の授業はどうでしょう．ぼくはとっても fun work だと思ってますけど．

SESSION 13

Barbie as a Second Language

■

Larry McCaffery

IF BARBIE'S NATIVE tongue is distinctly American, her dialect is decidedly Southern Californian. In the song "Valley Girl" by Frank Zappa, the dialect was satirized while making fun of the language distortions favored by teenage girls living in the San Fernando Valley — a region of Los Angeles. This is Barbie's birth- [5] place: near the beaches, Disneyland, and Hollywood. It seems the transient nature of California perfectly suits Barbie in her ongoing parade of costume, personality, and ethnicity changes.

Of course, Barbie shares this ability to transform herself with the other best-known female image among American women: [10] Madonna. And as has been true of Madonna, it has been Barbie's ability to be "consumed" by people in very different ways that has made her a perfect icon of postmodernism. Indeed, postmodernism and feminism seems to have converged in the figure of Barbie. Barbie is the subject of a book by M.G. Lord (*Forever Barbie*, 1994) and of a virtual mini-genre of poems, including [15] "Barbie's Ferrari" by Lynne McMahon and an entire sequence entitled *It's My Body* by Denise Duhamel.

Sales of Barbie dolls have never sagged, nor has Barbie herself, nor the fashion industry which she so inertly represents. With [20] periodic changes of hairstyle, clothes, and make-up, Barbie has maintained her mass appeal.

1970年代以来，アメリカ・ポストモダン作家研究の第一線に立ってきたラリー・マキャフリーとの出会いは，1981年のあるシンポジウムのときのこと．以来，お互い，日本とアメリカ，どっちがヘン(weird)かをめぐって，カセットやビデオを送り合ってきた．やや毛色の変わった「現在作家」のインタビュー集多数．日本では『アヴァン・ポップ』(筑摩書房)という本をまとめている．東大では一度ブルース・スプリングスティーンについての講演をやってもらった．「語学学習にもなるようなものを」と頼んだら，「第二外国語としてのバービー」という原稿を入れてくれるところが，いかにもラリーである．㋚

[1] her dialect: バービーのしゃべり方．松田聖子のブリッコ風の言葉と発声は，ハキハキ娘中尾ミエのとはちがっている．そしてそのちがいには，60年代と80年代で少女らの心の弾み，夢のトーンやリズムがどう移ってきたかが絡んでいる．

[3] Frank Zappa: 高貴なギターといかがわしいステージ．アメリカ文化を笑い皮肉り，ついには大統領候補にうって出て，そしてあっさり死んでしまった．これほど説明不能なロック・ミュージシャンが一体今後現われるだろうか．

[4] the San Fernando Valley: ビバリーヒルズの丘の北側，四方を山に囲まれた広い平地．幹線101号が通るあたりは巨大なビジネス・センターだ．

[6] the beaches, Disneyland, and Hollywood: バービーの誕生したのは，ビーチ・パーティとサーフィンが高校生に広まり，ディズニーランドが開園し，映画ではジェームス・ディーンら「反抗のアイドル」が人気を博した時代のこと．いわば気分，楽しさ感覚，夢，願望，カッコヨサのイメージといったものが，大きな商品価値をもって登場した時代である．

[7] her ongoing parade of costume, personality, and ethnicity changes: バービーちゃんは着せ替え人形．時代に応じ，気分に応じ，顧客の人種の別に応じて変身しながら「人格」までも変えてきたようすが，これから語られていく．

[13] a perfect icon of postmodernism: ポストモダンの時代は，(聖母と娼婦の間を軽々と飛びうつるマドンナのような)変幻自在のイメージの流動を特徴とする．バービーはそんな時代を完璧に象徴する偶像的存在というわけ．

[16] a virtual mini-genre of poems: “Barbie poems” が，それで1つの小ジャンルをなすほどの隆盛ぶりだということ．

[19] Sales of Barbie has never sagged: はじめて市場に出た1959年以来，これまでに作られたバービーは十億体に近づいている．バービーは人類を凌ぐか？
nor has Barbie herself: 誕生から数えればもう30代後半だけど，バービーはなんて「いつまでもピチピチ」(never sagged) なんだろう．

[20] inertly: 人形は「活動しない」(inert). 自分から服を選んだりはしない．

But what exactly does she do?

In a world of high technology, does Barbie even have a future?

Relax. To maintain her prestige, Barbie has changed her body mechanics many times. Her first overhaul came in 1967 with the "twist 'n' turn" Barbie, featuring life-like eyelashes and a rotating [5] waist. A more radical change occurred in 1971. Prompted by the Sexual Revolution, "Malibu Barbie" burst upon the scene and dropped her demure, side-long gaze in favor of a straight-ahead, *right-in-your-face* view.

This changing point of view adapted well to a cover-girl image [10] when "Fashion Photo Barbie" arrived on the toy store shelves. When a child focused a toy camera, Barbie went into action . . . striking poses worthy of *Vogue* and *Seventeen*. It wasn't long before Barbie was hanging out with Hollywood stars as Mattel unleashed all new Barbie versions of real-life celebrities, such as [15] Debby Boone, The Osmonds, and all three "Charlie's Angels," (Certainly *not* the rocker Frank Zappa.)

Yes, uptown Barbie comes "dressed to kill" in a startling array of languages and thought-provoking styles. Just check out the famed NYC toy store, F.A.O. Schwartz. Note the shrinking skirts, [20] stripes & leather worn by African-American Barbie, Native-American Barbie, Japanese Barbie, Mexican-American Barbie . . . .

[4] overhaul： ふつうは車等の分解修理に使う言葉.

[7] "Malibu Barbie"： ロス北西の海岸沿いのマリブは，ハリウッドスターがたくさん住んでいる憧れの高級住宅地.

[8] dropped her demure, side-long gaze in favor of a straight-ahead, *right-in-your-face* view： スイートにとりすましたお嬢さん的性格を棄てて，アグレッシブなイケイケ娘に変身したということを，目線の違いで表現した文.

[13] striking poses worthy of *Vogue* and *Seventeen*： 両誌とも女の子向けの代表的なファッション誌．19 世紀末に誕生した *Vogue* の方が格調も年齢層も高い．モデルのポーズが特に大胆というわけではないけれども，人形がそれをやるというと——日本の「リカちゃん」を思ってみたまえ——話は別.

[14] Mattel： ポーランド系の貧しい移民の娘ルース・ハンドラーが夫エリオットとつくったこの会社が，バービーによって世界一の玩具会社になったきっかけは，ヨーロッパの街角で見かけた「ふくよかな胸のお人形」だったそうな.

[16] Debby Boone： ロックンロールの創生期にソフトな声と甘いマスクで人気を得たパット・ブーンの娘は，やはり清純なイメージで 1977 年，「恋するデビー」(You Light Up My Life) の超ヒット(ビルボード 10 週連続トップ)を飛ばした.

The Osmonds： 70 年代初頭に盛り上がった家族バンド．ダニー坊やは「カルピスだ！」の宣伝にも大活躍.

"Charlie's Angels"： サラ・フォーセット・メジャーズら三人の美女が犯人を追跡する，「セーラー・ムーン」の原形となった(ウソ)，ポリス・アクションもの.

[18] uptown Barbie： uptown はニューヨークのミッドタウンからセントラル・パークにかけての地区を漠然と指す言葉．学生や移民，芸術家が多い downtown とは対照的に，店も高級志向であって，夜には最先端のファッションでリッチに決めた男女がガラスの煌(きら)めくドアをくぐる.

"dressed to kill"： 「ばっちり決めて」を意味する常套句．kill はこの場合「悩殺」の「殺」に近い意味．デ・パルマ監督は，それに文字どおりの意味をひっかけて，スリラー映画の名作の題名にした(邦題『殺しのドレス』).

a startling array of languages： バービーの「おしゃべり」の中にハッとするようなセリフがいっぱい入っているということ.

The hair, short and chic. Or long and luxurious. Or something anywhere in between. Sprayed, spiraled, streaked, tinted, twisted, teased, permed, curled, wound, wet. Nails glittered, glossed, lacquered, spattered, patterned. Softly muted baby-doll make-up and mesh tank tops, backpacks & belts, rayon & suede [5] worn with leather oxfords & soft-skin shoulder bags; Barbie is ready . . . as she has been for thirty-something years now . . . ready for her night on the town.

What will Barbie drive? It doesn't seem likely she would take the subway; too risky after dark. (Although Aikido Barbie might). [10] Yes, there is a Barbie with her own chauffeur, but why not her own set of car keys? Hence, the battery-powered Barbie-car. Automatic shift, forward & reverse, horns and high-beams (no car alarm yet). Big enough for a child, capable of handling those backyard bumps and slicks. Now that Barbie has her own [15] sportscar and hangs out with celebrities, you might wonder if somewhere along her rise to fame and autonomy, Ken got dumped. True, Ken was never quite the cultural icon; male figure dolls were traditionally the losers in the marketplace. Mattel knew all about it. In fact, they never wanted to produce Ken but [20] consumers pushed for a boyfriend-figure until they did. That was 1961 and Ken has sort of hung around ever since, escorting Barbie

[3] teased：逆毛を立ててふくらませる
wet：ムース等を塗ってしっとり濡れた感じを出す
Nails glittered, glossed, lacquered, spattered, patterned：マニュキアも煌めきのあるもの，光沢を出すもの，ベットリとエナメルカラーをかぶせるもの(lacquered)，不規則なポチポチ模様にしたり(spattered)，模様を描いたり，と多種多様．

[4] softly muted baby-doll makeup：ケバくなるのを抑え，赤ちゃんの人形のようなスベスベお肌に仕上げたメイク

[6] leather oxfords：皮のオックスフォード・シューズ

[7] as she has been for thirty-something years：誕生した時からバービーは，ファッショナブルにキメて，夜のお出かけをする用意ができていたということ．

[10] Aikido：アメリカ，特に西海岸ではカラテやテコンドーに次ぐ人気を保つ．

[12] set of car keys：アメリカではドア・キーとエンジン・キーはふつう別々だから，複数の車をもっているという意味は特に出ない．
Hence, . . .：というわけで〜の登場となる．
Automatic shift, forward and reverse：前方走行，後方走行ともオートマチックでギアが入る

[13] horns and high-beams：クラクションと遠方照射ヘッドライト
no car alarm yet：車の盗難が多いアメリカでは，他人がドアに手をかけるとけたたましくサイレンが鳴りだす装置が普及しているけれど，そういう現実は，まだバービー的な世界には反映されていない，ということ．

[15] backyard bumps and slicks：裏庭のデコボコも，滑りやすい路面も

[17] somewhere along her rise to fame and autonomy：名声と自立を勝ち得ていく過程で
got dumped：棄てられた; お役ごめんになった

[18] cultural icon：「文化偶像」と呼ばれるためには，単に優れているだけでは足らない．都はるみはOKでも，大月みやこは役不足．サリンジャーは○だが，ソール・ベローは×．山田邦子とビートたけしは○で，和田アキ子は△？

[21] until they did：until Mattel produced a boyfriend

[22] has sort of hung around：なんとなく居つづけてきた

to parties & getting her home before midnight. But is he just another handsome face with flawless physique and a sportscar? Now that Barbie comes with her own sportscar, maybe Ken will fade out of the picture . . . .

The new trends in menswear suggest Ken will stick around, [5] changing costumes faster than Superman. Wearing flashy colors, layers & berets, tweeds & suedes, sweaters & knits . . . even earrings and lavender vests. Still, there are fewer Kens than Barbies to flaunt the fashions. Maybe Ken needs a facelift. Barbie, however, retains her status as shapely, chic role model for another [10] generation of children attuned to glamour, movies, Hollywood. Even Ken would admit fashion isn't going out of style, but is it possible in a Post-Human Society, for Barbie to retain her popularity without changing her message?

Power to the B.L.O.

"Math is hard . . . " went the Barbie script, but her timeless [15] drone failed to cast the usual spell on hundreds of children across the country. It was Christmas 1993 and it looked as if the factories had made an amusing error. "Lets' go shopping!" chirped G.I. Joe, a macho action-figure doll for boys; while from Barbie's prim lips issued a string of military commands in the bellowing voice [20] of G.I. Joe.

Across the country, press releases announced the existence of the B.L.O. — the Barbie Liberation Organization. Tired of the banal gender stereotypes perpetuated by Mattel, this anonymous network of free-speak technicians had taken matters into their [25] own hands. Kidnapping Barbie and G.I. Joe from U.S. stores, they had then switched their voice boxes and smuggled the dolls back onto the shelves. Disrupting the predictable scripts may have bothered adults more than children, but Barbie is just *part* of the plan . . . . In the future, the organization intends to carry out other [30] well-orchestrated attacks on convention. The more things stay the

[1] just another: どこにでもいる，ありふれた一人の

[5] The new trends in menswear suggests . . . : イギリスとちがって木訥な伝統の強いアメリカでは,「男のおしゃれ」は80年代まで一般的には定着しなかった.
stick around: not disappear

[6] faster than Superman: スーパーマンといえば，“faster than a speeding bullet” というのが，おきまりの形容文句.

[7] layers: プレッピー・ファッションなどでやる「重ね着」

[9] flaunt: ひけらかす
facelift: 美容整形

[10] shapely, chic role model: 体型的にもおしゃれのセンスでも手本となる存在

[12] isn't going out of style: いつの世もなくなりはしない.

[13] Post-Human Society: コンピュータと人間が合体したサイバースペースの中では当然人間らしさも変化するというのが，たとえばラリーの友人，ブルース・スターリングのSF作家としての立場．バービーの変身を観察しながら，ラリー自身もポスト・ヒューマンな時代に向けての鼓動を感じているようだ.

Power to the B.L.O.: “Power to the people” をもじった闘争へのエール.

[15] the Barbie script: 「おしゃべりバービー」に仕込まれた(女の子っぽい)セリフ
timeless drone: どんなに時代が進んでも，まだ言っている退屈なセリフ

[16] the usual spell: 「いつもの魔法」とは，いわゆる女の子っぽい趣味やふるまいを植え付ける力のこと.

[18] chirp(ed): 甲高くさえずる．次の bellowing voice と対照的に使われている.
G.I. Joe: 日本でもおなじみ，マッテル社から出ている兵士人形.

[22] press releases: 報道関係者に対する発表

[23] B.L.O.: P.L.O. (Palestine Liberation Organization) のもじり.
Tired: 疲労ではなく，「いいかげんにしろ」という怒りの気持ちを表わす.

[24] perpetuate(d): いつまでも繰り返す

[25] free-speak technicians: 音声を細工して解放された言葉に変えてしまう人たち
take(n) matters into their own hands: (傍観をやめて)自分たちで事を起こす

[27] smuggled the dolls back onto the shelves: 店の棚にこっそり返す．B.L.O. の面々は「われわれは金を払ってバービーを買い込み，無料で棚に返している．犯罪者どころか，おもちゃ業界最高のお客さんなのだ」とうそぶいていた.

[31] The more things stay the same, the more the B.L.O. wants change: “The more things change, the more they stay the same” (変化することによってかえって変わらぬ部分が見えてくる)という諺がある．それをひっくり返して「とにかく変化を!」というのは，フムフム，やっぱりラリーだ.

same, the more the B.L.O. wants change . . . maybe as simple as a few cosmetic alterations.

In NY's Soho district, in a store where artists sell their creations — in this case their *re-creations* — Barbie is the artist's muse. But here it's more a picnic in Jurassic Park than Central Park, and the [5] vision of Hollywood comes closer to "Beverly Chills," for Barbie & Ken's date takes place at the General Hospital where Vampire Barbie gets liposuction to remove unwanted fat, while Asthmatic Ken is treated with oxygen & stitches after falling off his yacht and getting mauled by sharks. Accident-prone Barbie comes with [10] her own removable crutches, and third-degree burn victim Barbie has spent too long at the tanning parlor. Body-builder Ken is trapped beneath his giant weight machine, while Sweet Sixteen Barbie comes with her own car wreck. *Relax*. No one gets hurt.

Even in Soho, weight is a *big* issue. For Sumo Barbie comes in [15] two sizes, as well as both sexes. And there is no weight discrimination here; both Ken and Barbie come in 200 lb. and 400 lb. models. So lighten up — laugh — get used to the new proportions. Barbie's image is in the process of transformation.

[3] Soho： ニューヨークのダウンタウン，グリニッジ・ヴィレッジの南側 (South of Houston Street) の地区．戦後アメリカの前衛芸術の中心地．

[4] in this case their *re-creations*： オリジナルな作品ではなく，バービーというすでに創られたものをネタにしているから．以下にその作品例が並ぶ．

the artist's muse： 芸術家にインスピレーションを与える女神．

[6] "Beverly Chills"： 高級住宅地 Beverly Hills に，恐怖の戦慄を意味する chill をかけている．

[8] liposuction： 真空吸引器で皮下脂肪を除去する手術

Asthmatic： 喘息 (asthma) をわずらっている

[10] maul(ed)： ズタズタに引き裂く

Accident-prone Barbie comes with her own removable crutches： 「取り外し自在の松葉杖とセットで売っている」というのはサディスト趣味のお客用だろうか．accident-prone は「事故に遭いやすい」の意味．

[11] third-degree burn victim Barbie has spent too long at the tanning parlor： つまり，日焼けサロンで第三度(重傷)の火傷を負ったバービー．

[15] Even in Soho, weight is a *big* issue： 体重(体型)の話題は，エアロビ通いのおばさんか，低俗なタブロイド誌の話かと思いきや．．．．なお，big の強調は，作品の巨大さという意味がかけられているから．

[17] come in 200 lb. and 400 lb. models： 200 ポンド(舞の海クラス)と 400 ポンド(水戸泉クラス)，2 通りの品揃えがある．バービーを太らすというのは，現代イメージ＝ファッション＝健康文化への，かなり露骨な挑戦だ．

SESSION 14

Ella's Special Camera

■

David Blair

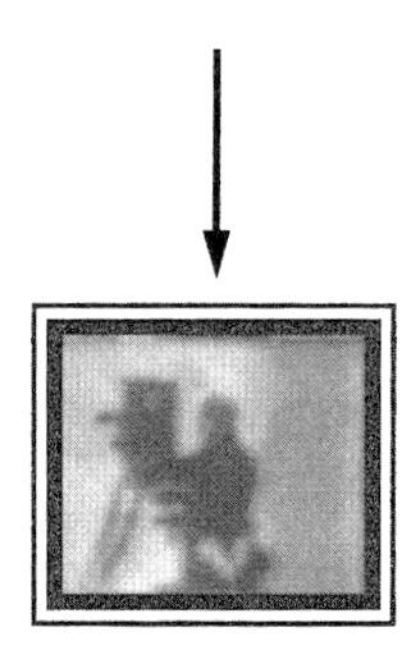

From WAXWEB, a hypertext version of the video
WAX, OR THE DISCOVERY OF TELEVISION AMONG THE BEES

「電子映画」製作の一方でデイヴィッド・ブレアは，インターネットを活用した“観客”との新しい関係のあり方も模索する．1991年に映画館で初演され，東京でも上演されて話題となった『WAX：蜜蜂TVの発見』は，まもなくその全編がインターネットに載った(長編映像作品としては世界初)．現在では数千枚のカラー・スチールと何カ国語ものサウンドトラックをハイパーテクストで結び合わせた，ヴァーチャル・ストーリー・サイトを形成している．**http://www.waxweb.org** へ．

図書館でテーマ・リサーチしながら，映像アーカイブで関係資料(フィルムや写真)を探し当て，見つかったものをもとに映像的展開を組立て，できるだけ金を使わずに機材を調達し，制作奨励金を切らさないようにしながら脚本を書き進み，演出と撮影を(時には主演も)同時にこなし，デジタル編集で仮想現実の世界を展開させながらふたたび筋書き自体を再構成する．しかもビデオ制作とインターネット・サイトづくりを同時並行的に進める．1作仕上げるのに10年かかろうと知らん顔という仕事ぶりだ．東大駒場の客員教授(表象文化論)も歴任．現在はパリ近郊に住み，デジタル絵巻巨編 *Lost Tribes* の完成を目指している．㊚

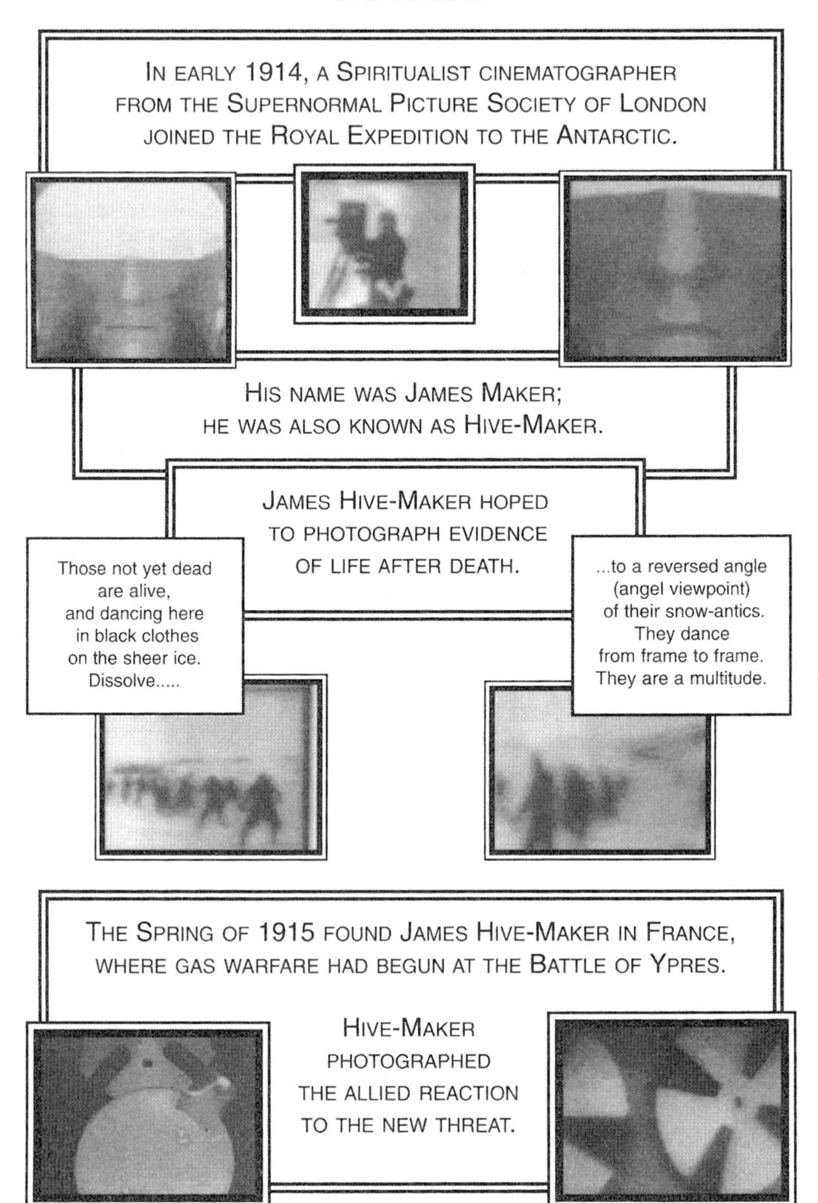
ELLA'S SPECIAL CAMERA
FROM WAXWEB, AN INTERNET/CDROM VERSION OF THE MOVIE "WAX"
BY DAVID BLAIR
IN EARLY 1914, A SPIRITUALIST CINEMATOGRAPHER
FROM THE SUPERNORMAL PICTURE SOCIETY OF LONDON
JOINED THE ROYAL EXPEDITION TO THE ANTARCTIC.
HIS NAME WAS JAMES MAKER;
HE WAS ALSO KNOWN AS HIVE-MAKER.
JAMES HIVE-MAKER HOPED
TO PHOTOGRAPH EVIDENCE
OF LIFE AFTER DEATH.
Those not yet dead
are alive,
and dancing here
in black clothes
on the sheer ice.
Dissolve.....
...to a reversed angle
(angel viewpoint)
of their snow-antics.
They dance
from frame to frame.
They are a multitude.
THE SPRING OF 1915 FOUND JAMES HIVE-MAKER IN FRANCE,
WHERE GAS WARFARE HAD BEGUN AT THE BATTLE OF YPRES.
HIVE-MAKER
PHOTOGRAPHED
THE ALLIED REACTION
TO THE NEW THREAT.

本文で大文字の箇所はナレーション(のすべて)，小さい文字のところは ***Waxweb*** に載っている映像解説(の一部)．

Spiritualist cinematographer： 霊の映像を撮影する専門家

Supernormal Picture Society： 「超常写真学会」．supernormal は「すごくノーマル」ではなく「ノーマルを超えた」．当時イギリスでは，いわゆるオカルト・サイエンスが盛り上がり，実在したこの会にも科学者を含む著名人が参加していた．

Royal Expedition to the Antarctic： スコット隊長が率いた英国探検隊の南極点への到達はこの 2 年前に達成されている．

Hive-Maker： 大文字の Maker には「創造主」の意味がある．hive は「蜂の巣」だが，この物語では「現実」に隣接する死の映像世界全体の象徴となっている．被写体は作家ウィリアム・バロウズ．デイヴィッドはカンザスに彼を訪ね，蜜蜂用ネットをかぶせて撮影した．

Those not yet dead . . . are dancing： 「死の舞踏」はこの作品の基本映像モチーフ．死者たちが謎めいた文字となって踊るところは特に印象的だ．

the sheer ice： 一面の氷の世界

Dissolve： 「ディゾルブ」とは，2 つの場面が重なりながら漸次入れ替わる方法．

reversed angle (angel viewpoint)： 逆方向(高い位置)からのショット．天使のように上から見下ろすショットを angel (angelic) shot という．

snow-antics： 雪上の狂態．左のスチールにフレームが見えるが，ここの部分は映画フィルムを 1 コマずつビデオで撮影するという手法をとっている．行進の動きの異様さ・滑稽さを浮き立たせる編集だ．

The spring of 1915 found James Hive-Maker in France： 時や場所を主語に，see や find を動詞にして出来事を記す書き方．12 ページ 32 行目，68 ページ 17 行目参照．

gas warfare： 「毒ガス戦」だけでなく，この電子映画では原爆やミサイルのシミュレーターなどが，「死の王国」の侵入として描かれる．この点はトマス・ピンチョンの小説の影響が濃厚だ．『重力の虹』はデイヴィッドの一番の愛読書．

Ypres： [íːprə] ベルギーのフランス国境近くの町．第一次大戦では三たび激戦場に．

the Allied [əláid, ǽlaid] reaction： 連合国側の反応

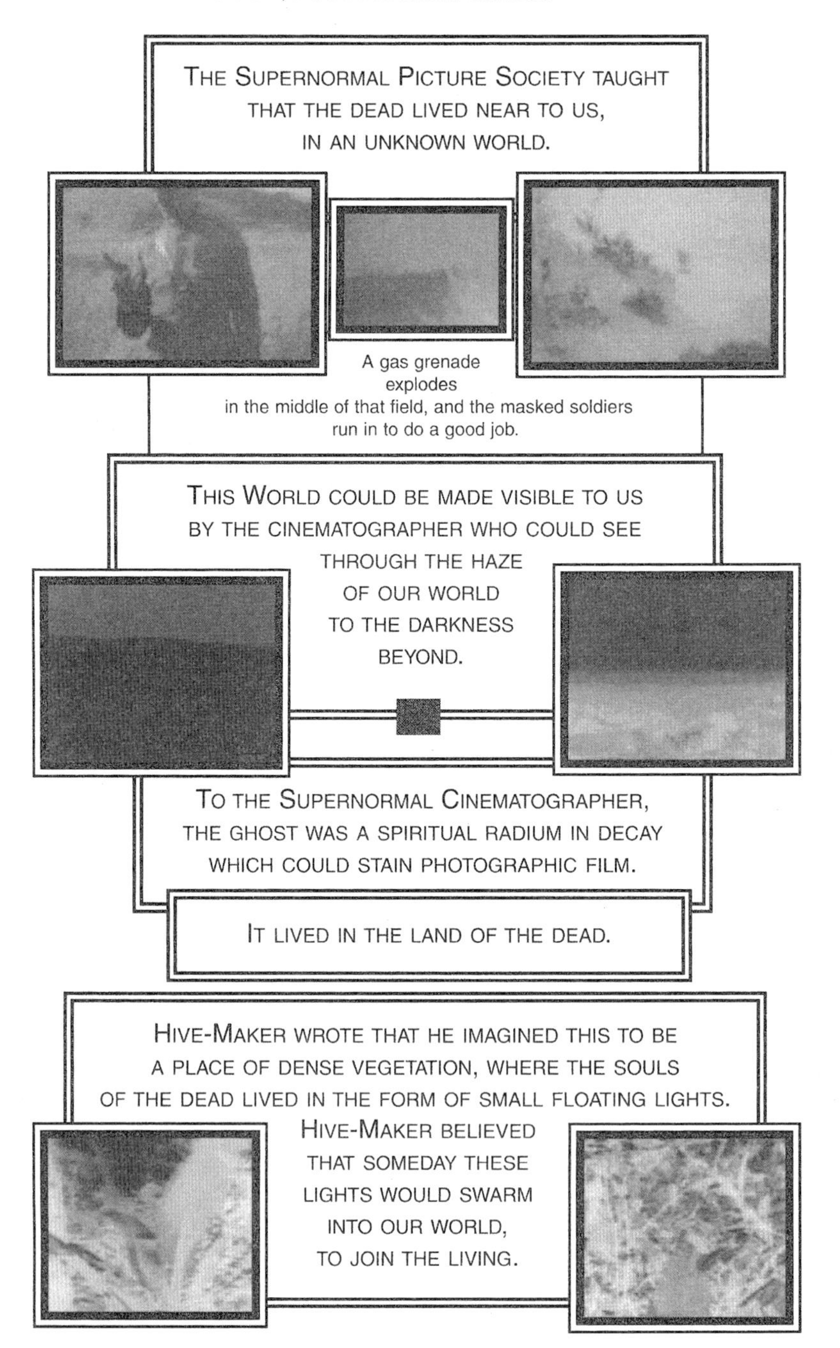
The Supernormal Picture Society taught that the dead lived near to us, in an unknown world.
A gas grenade explodes in the middle of that field, and the masked soldiers run in to do a good job.
This World could be made visible to us by the cinematographer who could see through the haze of our world to the darkness beyond.
To the Supernormal Cinematographer, the ghost was a spiritual radium in decay which could stain photographic film.
It lived in the land of the dead.
Hive-Maker wrote that he imagined this to be a place of dense vegetation, where the souls of the dead lived in the form of small floating lights.
Hive-Maker believed that someday these lights would swarm into our world, to join the living.

gas grenade : [grənéid] 毒ガス散布用手榴弾

run in to do a good job : ここで 4 人の兵士が走り込んできて見事に手榴弾を投げるシーンが映される．その爆発に続いて暗転．3 秒後その暗黒に，ぼんやりとした星型の図形が現われ，それがはじける．(以後もたびたび現われるこの図形が「死の国」に属するのだという連想が，このような並置からしだいに僕たちの心にできあがってくる．)

the darkness beyond : ここで画面は左ページ左中央の暗い風景写真から，右側のネガティブ(白黒反転映像)に移行する．現実(生者の国)とパラレルに存在する死者の国を表現する技法である．このページの下の 2 枚もネガ．

a spiritual radium in decay : 朽ちかけた霊的放射線

the land of the dead : 月や地中にある死者の国に，ブレア本人が演じる「私」(Hive-Maker の孫，Jacob Maker)が連れていかれる(または頭に埋め込まれた蜜蜂 TV 受像機を通して，そこに連れていかれた映像を体験する)シーンが出てくる．

place of dense vegetation : 植生豊かな地

swarm into : ～に蜂の集団のように押し寄せる．swarm という語によって，次ページに登場する「蜂」が，死者の国からの使いであることが示唆される．実は，映像的に言うと，「植物」から「蜂」に至る途中が一番おもしろい．一瞬地平線上に一人の男が小さく見えたかと思うと，次の瞬間，さきほど現われた星型図形が再登場，その作用で(?)男が一瞬にして増殖したかのように，同じ白い夜空のもとに，群衆 (a swarm of people) が現われ出る．と突然，古代エジプトの死のマスク(石像)が 1 秒間に 10 体ほどの圧倒的なスピードで照射され，画面はふたたび映写機に嚙み込まれるフィルムの映像に戻る．詳しくは ビデオまたは *Waxweb* を見てください．

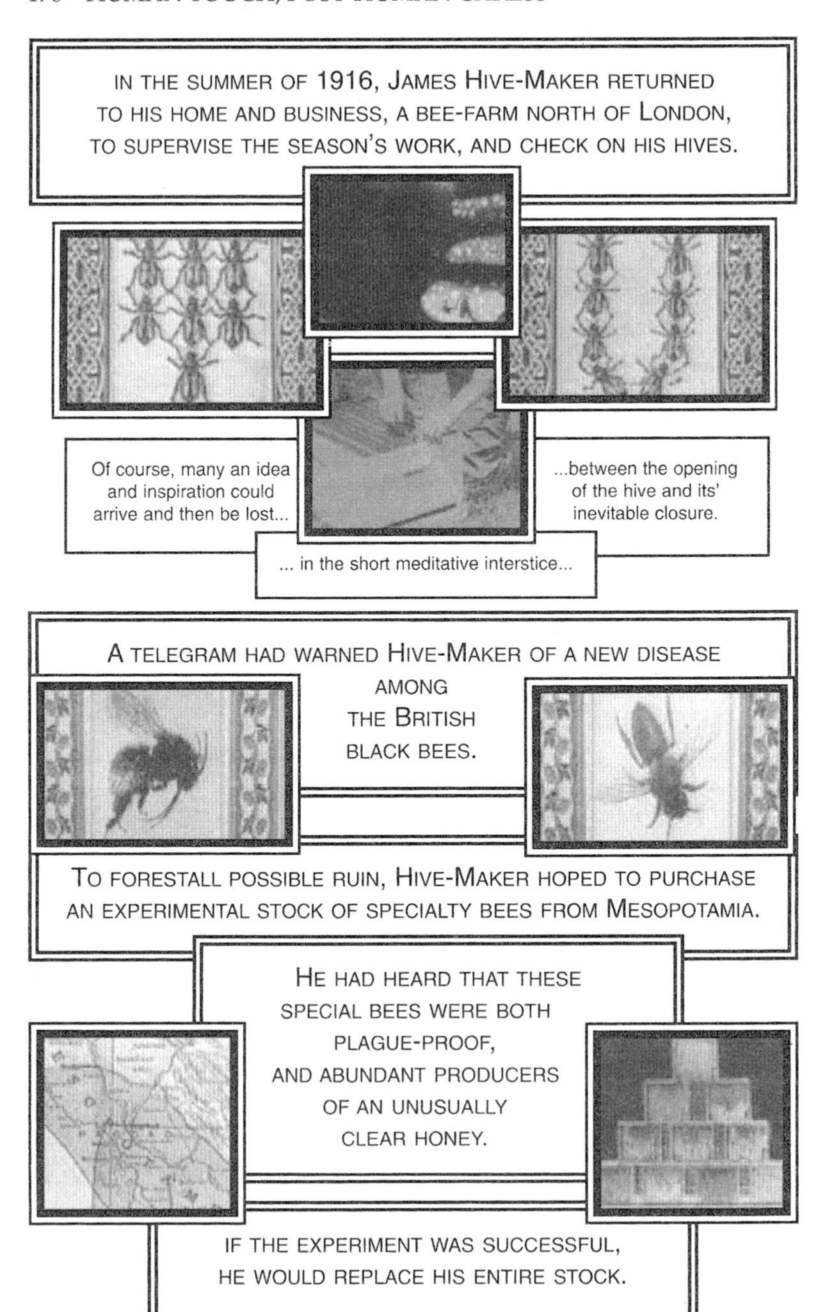
IN THE SUMMER OF 1916, JAMES HIVE-MAKER RETURNED TO HIS HOME AND BUSINESS, A BEE-FARM NORTH OF LONDON, TO SUPERVISE THE SEASON'S WORK, AND CHECK ON HIS HIVES.
Of course, many an idea and inspiration could arrive and then be lost...
... in the short meditative interstice...
...between the opening of the hive and its' inevitable closure.
A TELEGRAM HAD WARNED HIVE-MAKER OF A NEW DISEASE AMONG THE BRITISH BLACK BEES.
TO FORESTALL POSSIBLE RUIN, HIVE-MAKER HOPED TO PURCHASE AN EXPERIMENTAL STOCK OF SPECIALTY BEES FROM MESOPOTAMIA.
HE HAD HEARD THAT THESE SPECIAL BEES WERE BOTH PLAGUE-PROOF, AND ABUNDANT PRODUCERS OF AN UNUSUALLY CLEAR HONEY.
IF THE EXPERIMENT WAS SUCCESSFUL, HE WOULD REPLACE HIS ENTIRE STOCK.

its inevitable closure : 「避けがたき巣箱の閉鎖」.「避けがたき」という思わせぶりの言葉で何をいわんとしているのか——そしてその前の medetative interstice (つかの間の省察の時) とは何なのか——この段階ではまだよくわからない. 巣箱を開けて蜂と交わる時間は, 何か日常とは切れた, 霊的な交感のようなことが起こる時だという感じが, 漠然とするだけだ.

forestall possible ruin : 万一の倒産を未然に防ぐ

purchase an experimental stock of specialty bees : 特別な資質をもった蜂を試験的に買い込む

plague-proof : 疫病にかからない

〈**真ん中最上部のスチール**〉: 前ページの最後の注で描写したシークエンスが暗転したのち, すぐこの映像に入る. 画面右側に見えるのはレンズに触れた人間の指. これが取り除かれると木々の前を天に昇っていく小さな(すでに不吉な)光の水玉が現われ, ディゾルブの後, 今度はその水玉の背景に, Hive-Maker の家らしきものが現われる.

〈**右下のスチール**〉: 闇を背景に, 蜜蜂の巣箱が積み上げられている. ここに流れるのが "if the experiment was successful . . . " というナレーション. 蜜のつまった箱が積み上がったこのイメージは, 一応のところ事業成功のシンボルだといえる. (でも不吉なことに, 後に重要なモチーフの一つになるバベルの塔にもよく似ている.)

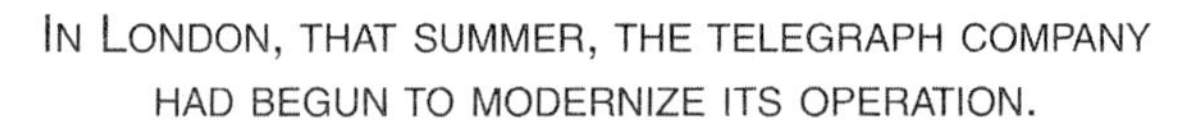

IN LONDON, THAT SUMMER, THE TELEGRAPH COMPANY
HAD BEGUN TO MODERNIZE ITS OPERATION.

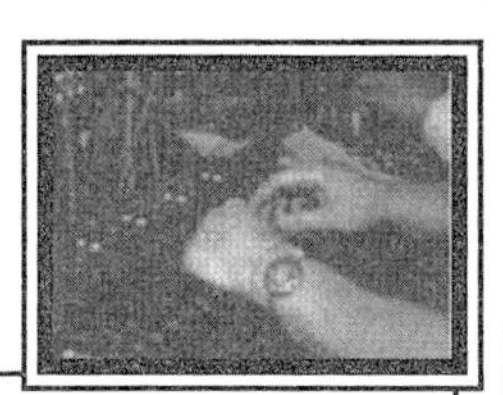

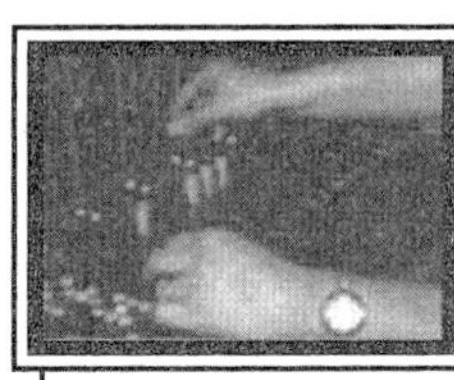

A high shot of camera-memorized workers thrashing at a switchboard, patching though calls from the dead of the future. Among them is (are)...

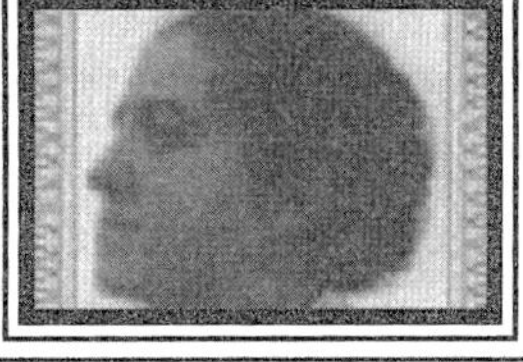

...Ella, a slow but certain genius...

...who understands the potentialities of hybridity in the construction of those systems neccessary to connect us with those we love.

AS A RESULT, ELLA SPIRALUM LOST HER JOB AS A TELEPHONE OPERATOR.

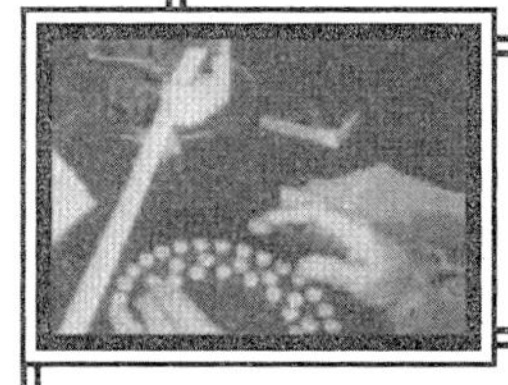

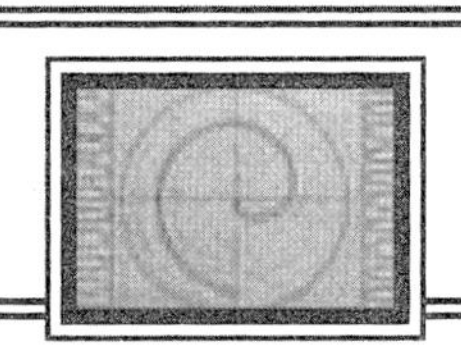

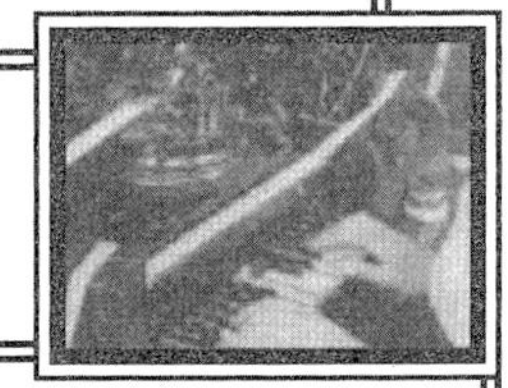

IRONICALLY, SPIRALUM WAS HERSELF AN ELECTRICAL INVENTOR, WHO DREAMED OF DEVELOPING THE MEANS TO TRANSMIT MOVING PICTURES THROUGH THE TELEPHONE.

A still frontal image of the always rotating Nipkow Disk, central and metal-made component of an Image Dissecting system proposed in the 1880"s, by a Berlin student...

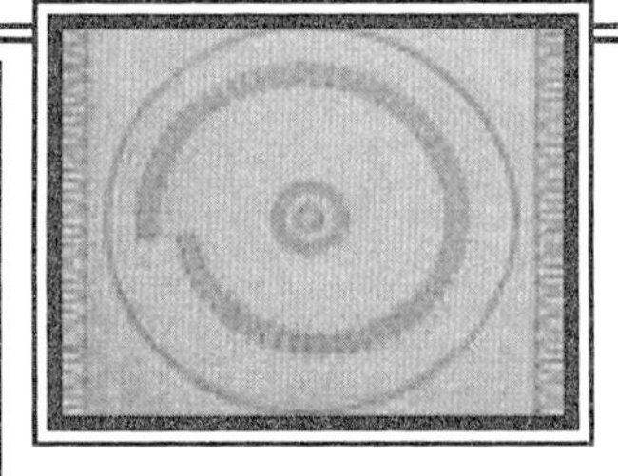

This winding gyre, once used to accurately slice coherent sections of our world for single transmission and multiple reception, is now part of history.

...who in later years was proclaimed by Adolf Hitler to be the Father of Television.

camera-memorized workers : 「カメラによって記憶された労働者」というのは奇妙な言い方だが，昔の映像を見ていると，この人たちはたぶん今はもう死んでいて，ただ「カメラ」を通して保存されているだけにすぎないという感覚がしてくるのは事実だ．

thrash(ing) at : ～を勢いよく叩く

patch(ing) through : (回線)を接続する

Among them is (are) : もちろん常識的には主語がEllaなのだからisが正しい．ただこの物語世界では，一人の人間が多数の存在に分解したりすることも起こる．実際，ブレア自身が演じる語り手Jacob Makerは，ある時点でElla (の分身の一人)に姿を変える．

a slow but certain genius : 80年前の写真みたいに見せかけて，この写真の人は実は奥さんのフロレンス．(デイヴィッド自身にもあてはまりそうな)このユーモラスな賛辞は，きっと心からのものにちがいない．

hybridity : ここでいう「異種交配」とは，生者の交信回路に，死者との交信を混ぜること．

those we love : 「故人」を意味する "loved one(s)" と同じ意味．

Ella Spiralum : 発音は [élə spəlɔ́:ləm]．spiralは「渦巻き」で，それは次に出てくるNipkow Diskのイメージと呼応する．

transmit moving pictures through the telephone : デイヴィッドが *Waxweb* でやろうとしているのがまさにこれ．いま動画伝達の領域では1920年代以来続いた，無線 (television) 方式の支配が崩れつつある．

still frontal image : 正面からの静止画像

Nipkow Disk : ニプコー盤．渦巻き上に並んだ小さな正方形の穴から入ってくる光のそれぞれが電気信号に置き換えられて伝達される．この渦巻きが回転することで，被写体の全体がスキャンされることになる．まだ学生だったPaul Gottlieb Nipkowが1884年に発明．

Dissect(ing) : 開析する; 分析のために切りとる

winding gyre : 螺旋(渦巻)状の旋回物

slice coherent sections of our world : われわれの世界を(バラバラにではなく)筋の通った形に切りとる

for single transmission and multiple reception : ニプコー盤を組み入れた画像伝達システムは，それぞれの穴を通して得られた情報を個別に転送し (single transmission)，受信の側でそれを統合する (multiple reception) しくみになっていた．

Ella Spiralum was the half-sister of James Hive-Maker.

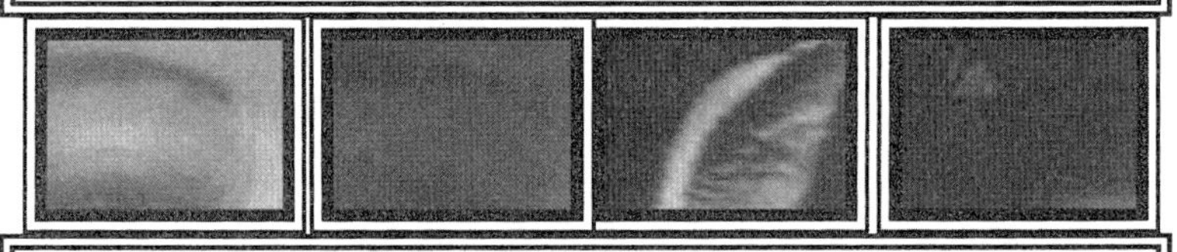

Through Hive-Maker, Ella Spiralum found work as
a photographic medium at the Supernormal Picture Society.

Flapping pictures of birds created by a clay-pigeon zoetrope at the Kensington Museum in London... large earth-made bird statues in various sequential poses are mounted in a giant horizontal drum with evenly spaced viewing slits cut in its side. When the drum is spun, the birds seem to become a single flying bird held in the eternal return of cycle animation (no mutation possible there in that machine-gunned eternal claylife, though the viewer is invited to wink and blink and use all manner of organic filters. in an attempt to create a new, unique, and, most importantly, surviveable and potentially reproducable image.)

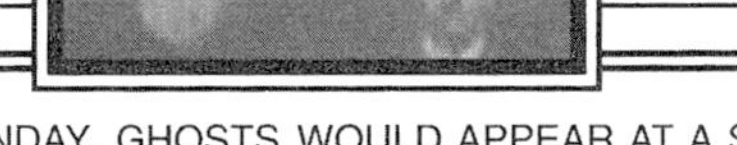

Each Sunday, ghosts would appear at a seance
in Tavistock Square, to be photographed with the living
by Ella and her special camera.

Photo of a cotton-garbed ectoplasm who has been mourned though the use of photography, but has minimal personality beyond its recallable face. To obtain such a ghost-picture, the mourner would visit the photo-medium. The medium would request to see a picture of the recently dead, in order to focus the concentration and energy to make a new exposure of this dead person on vaction in the other world. During this moment of concentration, the photo-medium would secretely rephotograph the picture of the formerly alive and still loved dead person. Then, for an extra charge, the medium would take a studio portrait of the mourner. The mourner would then depart, to return in a week to pay for a picture of the ghost, garbed-in-cotton ectoplasm, and also a two shot of the cotton ghost compositely posed with the still alive, recently recorded mourner.

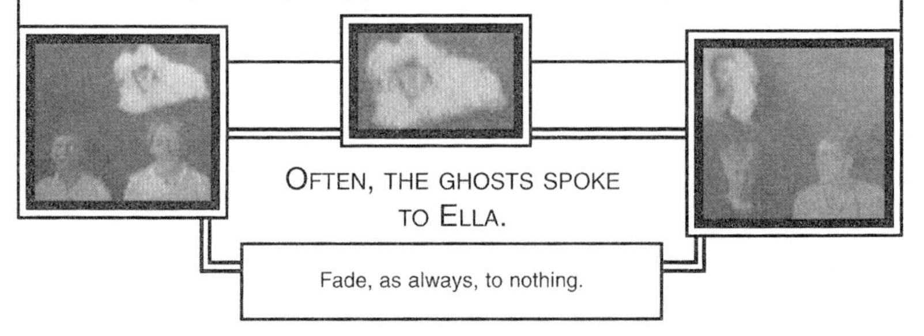

Often, the ghosts spoke
to Ella.
Fade, as always, to nothing.

photographic medium： 心霊写真の霊媒．後に登場する「蜜蜂 TV」も死の国からのヴァーチャル映像を運ぶ媒体 (medium) である．

clay-pigeon： ふつうは「クレイ射撃で使う素焼のディスク」のことだが，ここでは文字どおり素焼 (earth-made) の鳩の像．

zoetrope： [zóuitròup] ゾーエトロープ．たくさんの等間隔のスリットがある円筒の内側に，連続した運動を分解した各コマの絵が順番に描かれていて，円筒が回るとスリットを通してそれが動画として見えるようになっている．ここに出てくるのは，絵の代わりに飛ぶ鳥の立体像を使った巨大なもの．

held in the eternal return of cycle animation： 円筒が回る限り，鳥は永遠に同じ羽ばたき運動に捕らえられる．eternal return（永劫回帰）といっても最終的な安住の地はなく，輪廻の苦闘が続くばかり．

mutation： 突然変異．哀しき囚われの生を断ち切って別の存在に移行すること．mutation のあとに is を補うと完全な文になる．

that machine-gunned eternal claylife： "clay-pigeon" はそもそもガンで撃たれるべき存在．clay（土くれ）も「土に還る」という表現があるように，死を想起させる言葉．エラのクロースアップの顔に重ね合わされる鳩の羽ばたきには，死のイメージが何重にも塗り込まれている．

the viewer is invited to wink and blink . . .： 回転するゾーエトロープの前に立って瞬きをすると，われわれの瞼が，一種の生物的フィルター (organic filter) として働いて映像の動きが変化する．瞼の動きをうまくコントロールすることで，その新しい動きを保っておく (survive させる) ことも可能．

séance： 降霊会

Tavistock Square： ロンドンの一画

cotton-garbed： 綿の衣装を着た．（下段の写真参照）

ectoplasm： 「心霊体」．死者との交信中，霊媒の体から怪しく発するボワーっとした白いもの．あるいは，ボッと浮かんだ死者の霊．

mourn(ed)： （死者）を哀悼する

beyond its recallable face： 現世に呼び戻せる顔以外には

photo-medium： 「心霊写真館」とでも訳すのだろうか．「写真メディア」の意味でもある．

make a new exposure： 「新たに顕現させる」の意味と「新しくフィルムに収める」の意味がブレンドされている．

compositely： 写真合成によって．なお *Waxweb* のこの部分には全部で 8 枚の心霊写真のスチールが，解説付きでのっています．

SESSION 15

The Debutante

■

Leonora Carrington

WHEN I WAS A DEBUTANTE, I often went to the zoo. I went so often that I knew the animals better than I knew girls of my own age. Indeed it was in order to get away from people that I found myself at the zoo every day. The animal I got to know best was a young hyena. She knew me too. She was very [5] intelligent. I taught her French, and she, in return, taught me her language. In this way we passed many pleasant hours.

My mother was arranging a ball in my honour on the first of May. During this time I was in a state of great distress for whole nights. I've always detested balls, especially when they are given [10] in my honour.

On the morning of the first of May 1934, very early, I went to visit the hyena.

"What a bloody nuisance," I said to her. "I've got to go to my ball tonight." [15]

"You're very lucky," she said. "I'd love to go. I don't know how to dance, but at least I could make small talk."

"There'll be a great many different things to eat," I told her. "I've seen truckloads of food delivered to our house."

"And you're complaining," replied the hyena, disgusted. "Just [20] think of me, I eat once a day, and you can't imagine what a heap of bloody rubbish I'm given."

リオノーラ・キャリントンは1917年イギリスに生まれ，早くから絵画の才能を発揮した．やがてフランスにわたって，シュルレアリスムの寵児マックス・エルンストと同棲．第二次大戦が激化し，ドイツ系であるエルンストが拘留されるとショックで精神に異常をきたし，精神病院に入れられる．やがて回復してアメリカにわたり，1943年からメキシコに住んで，絵画，彫刻，タペストリーなどの活動に携わるとともに，メキシコの女性解放運動の先駆者としても活躍．小説は奇想天外，グロテスクなユーモアにあふれている．🅛

The Debutante : debutanteとは，社交界にデビューしようとしている若い令嬢のこと(「そんな話，興味ねえなあ」と思わず，まず最初の段落を読んでみてください)．かつてcome outといえばdebutanteが社交界にデビューすることを指したが(*Is Mrs. Brown's daughter coming out this year?*)，いまではむしろ，自分がゲイであることを宣言するという意味の“come out of the closet”の省略表現. *With all the talk about gay liberation, sometimes it's still not easy to come out.*

[4] The animal I got to know best : get toは「〜するようになる」

[5] hyena : ハイエナといえば①腐肉を食う，②(興奮すると)人間のように「笑う」という動物，というのが一般的イメージ．“laugh like a hyena”といえば，もちろん愛らしい笑いではない．

[8] was arranging a ball in my honour on the first of May : 「私のために5月1日に舞踏会を計画してくれていた」．5月1日は伝統的に春の到来を告げる日といわれ，first of Mayという言い方も一種の決まり文句．ビー・ジーズのヒット曲“First of May”には，「若葉のころ」というピッタリの邦題がついていた．

[9] distress : agony; suffering

[10] detested : hated. きわめて強い憎悪の表現.

[14] “What a bloody nuisance” : 「ほんとにやんなっちゃうわよ」．bloodyはイギリス英語ではきわめてポピュラーな罵りの言葉．“What do you mean by one man, one vote?” “Why! it means ‘one bloody man, one bloody vote.’” “Then why the hell don't they bloody well say so?” (「一人一票たあ何のこつたい.」「もち，一人の野郎に一枚(めえ)つてことよ.」「そんならそうと何故吐かしやがらねえんだ.」)——中島文雄『英語の常識』(研究社)．nuisanceは「厄介」

[17] small talk : 雑談，おしゃべり．*John doesn't waste time making small talk — he comes straight to the point.*

[19] truckloads of food : トラック何台分もの食べ物

[22] rubbish : ゴミ

I had an audacious idea, and I almost laughed. "All you have to do is to go instead of me!"

"We don't resemble each other enough, otherwise I'd gladly go," said the hyena rather sadly.

"Listen," I said. "No one sees too well in the evening light. If [5] you disguise yourself, nobody will notice you in the crowd. Besides, we're practically the same size. You're my only friend, I beg you to do this for me."

She thought this over, and I knew that she really wanted to accept. [10]

"Done," she said all of a sudden.

There weren't many keepers about, it was so early in the morning. I opened the cage quickly, and in a very few moments we were out in the street. I hailed a taxi; at home, everybody was still in bed. In my room I brought out the dress I was to wear that [15] evening. It was a little long, and the hyena found it difficult to walk in my high-heeled shoes. I found some gloves to hide her hands, which were too hairy to look like mine. By the time the sun was shining into my room, she was able to make her way around the room several times, walking more or less upright. We were so [20] busy that my mother almost opened the door to say good morning before the hyena had hidden under my bed.

"There's a bad smell in your room," my mother said, opening the window. "You must have a scented bath before tonight, with my new bath salts." [25]

"Certainly," I said.

She didn't stay long. I think the smell was too much for her.

"Don't be late for breakfast," she said and left the room.

The greatest difficulty was to find a way of disguising the hyena's face. We spent hours and hours looking for a way, but [30] she always rejected my suggestions. At last she said, "I think I've found the answer. Have you got a maid?"

"Yes," I said, puzzled.

"There you are then. Ring for your maid, and when she comes in we'll pounce upon her and tear off her face. I'll wear her face [35]

[1] audacious : 大胆な，無謀な

[7] practically : almost

You're my only friend : ハイエナに向かって You're my only friend と言うようなデビュタントがいたら，僕も友だちになりたい．

[11] Done : agreed

[12] There weren't many keepers about : あたりには飼育係もあまりいなかった

[19] make her way around the room several times : 部屋を何周かする

[20] more or less upright : まあ一応まっすぐ立って

[24] scented : 香水入りの

[32] Have you got . . . : Do you have のイギリス式表現.

[34] There you are then : じゃあそれで決まりよ

Ring for your maid : (ベルを鳴らして)女中を呼んでちょうだい

[35] pounce upon her and tear off her face : 飛びかかって顔をはぎ取る

tonight instead of mine."

"It's not practical," I said. "She'll probably die if she hasn't got a face. Somebody will certainly find the corpse, and we'll be put in prison."

"I'm hungry enough to eat her," the hyena replied. [5]

"And the bones?"

"As well," she said. "So, it's on?"

"Only if you promise to kill her before tearing off her face. It'll hurt her too much otherwise."

"All right. It's all the same to me." [10]

Not without a certain amount of nervousness I rang for Mary, my maid. I certainly wouldn't have done it if I didn't hate having to go to a ball so much. When Mary came in I turned to the wall so as not to see. I must admit it didn't take long. A brief cry, and it was over. While the hyena was eating, I looked out the window. [15] A few minutes later she said, "I can't eat any more. Her two feet are left over still, but if you have a little bag, I'll eat them later in the day."

"You'll find a bag embroidered with fleurs-de-lis in the cupboard. Empty out the handkerchiefs you'll find inside, and take [20] it." She did as I suggested. Then she said, "Turn round now and look how beautiful I am."

In front of the mirror, the hyena was admiring herself in Mary's face. She had nibbled very neatly all around the face so that what was left was exactly what was needed. [25]

"You've certainly done that very well." I said.

Towards evening, when the hyena was all dressed up, she declared, "I really feel in tip-top form. I have a feeling that I shall be a great success this evening."

When we had heard the music from downstairs for quite some [30] time, I said to her, "Go on down now, and remember, don't stand next to my mother. She's bound to realise that it isn't me. Apart from her I don't know anybody. Best of luck." I kissed her as I left her, but she did smell very strong.

Night fell. Tired by the day's emotions, I took a book and sat [35]

[3] Somebody will certainly find the corpse, and we'll be put in prison : と言っているが，発覚してもハイエナはたぶん刑務所には入れられないと思う．

[5] I'm hungry enough to eat her : ここで，ハイエナがハイエナであることが生きてくる．「ハイエナは人声をまねできるともいわれ，人の名を呼んで外へおびきだしては食い殺すと恐れられた．これはその独特な鳴声に由来する．また，腐肉をあさることから墓をあばいて死体を食う食屍鬼と同一視され，貪欲の象徴ともなっている」（荒俣宏，『平凡社世界大百科事典』）

[7] So, it's on? : じゃ，決まりね？

[8] Only if you promise to kill her before . . . : 優しいんだか残酷なんだか，よくわかりませんね．

[19] a bag embroidered with fleurs-de-lis : 白ユリの紋を刺繡したバッグ

[24] nibble(d) : （少しずつ）かじり取る

[28] tip-top : excellent; of the highest quality

[33] Best of luck : 日本語なら「がんばってね」か．

down by the open window, giving myself up to peace and quiet. I remember that I was reading *Gulliver's Travels* by Jonathan Swift. About an hour later, I noticed the first signs of trouble. A bat flew in at the window, uttering little cries. I am terribly afraid of bats. I hid behind a chair, my teeth chattering. I had hardly gone down [5] on my knees when the sound of beating wings was overcome by a great noise at my door. My mother entered, pale with rage.

"We'd just sat down at table," she said, "when that thing sitting in your place got up and shouted, 'So I smell a bit strong, what? Well, I don't eat cakes!' Whereupon it tore off its face [10] and ate it. And with one great bound, disappeared through the window."

[1] giving myself up to : ～に身をゆだねて

[2] *Gulliver's Travels* : 大人も子供も読む有名な本だが，中身はけっこう作者の厭人的な面が出ている．そのへんが，この人間嫌いハイエナ好きのデビュタントを惹きつけるのかも．

[5] I had hardly gone down on my knees when . . . : 私が(へなへなと)両膝をついたとたん～した

[8] We'd just sat down at table . . . when . . . : みんな食卓についたと思ったら，～した

[9] So I smell a bit strong, what? . . . : ふん，あたしがちょっとくらい臭うからって，何だってのよ？ こっちはケーキ食べて生きてるんじゃないんだからね！

[10] Whereupon : そこで，そう言って

柴田元幸＋佐藤良明（しばた・もとゆき/さとう・よしあき）
東大の英語教師．学年統一授業〈英語 I〉の教科書『The Universe of English』『The Expanding Universe of English』の編集主幹役をつとめる．共著に『佐藤君と柴田君』（白水社），共編著に『ロック・ピープル 101』（新書館）と放送大学教材『英語 VII』（'97–'00）（放送大学教育振興会）．ソロワークとして ㋛『生半可な學者』（白水社 U ブックス），『アメリカ文学のレッスン』（講談社現代新書），㋚『ラバーソウルの弾みかた』（平凡社ライブラリー），『J-POP 進化論』（平凡社新書）などがある．

The Parallel Universe of English

1996 年 12 月 20 日　初　版
2004 年 4 月 20 日　第 5 刷

［検印廃止］

編　者　佐藤良明・柴田元幸

発行所　財団法人　東京大学出版会

代 表 者　五 味 文 彦
113–8654 東京都文京区本郷 7 東大構内
電話 03–3811–8814・FAX 03–3812–6958
振替 00160–6–59964

印刷所　研究社印刷株式会社
製本所　株式会社島崎製本

ISBN 4–13–082102–4　Printed in Japan

本書はデジタル印刷機を採用しており、品質の経年変化についての充分なデータはありません。そのため高湿下で強い圧力を加えた場合など、色材の癒着・剥落・磨耗等の品質変化の可能性もあります。

The Parallel Universe of English

2023年9月5日　発行　②

編　者　佐藤良明・柴田元幸
発行所　一般財団法人　東京大学出版会
代 表 者　吉見俊哉
〒153-0041
東京都目黒区駒場4-5-29
TEL03-6407-1069　FAX03-6407-1991
URL　http://www.utp.or.jp/
印刷・製本　大日本印刷株式会社
URL　http://www.dnp.co.jp/

ISBN978-4-13-009138-1
Printed in Japan